THE IMPACT OF

Early Art Experiences on Literacy Development

Kathy Danko-McGhee & Ruslan Slutsky

About NAEA

The National Art Education Association is the world's largest professional art education association and a leader in educational research, policy, and practice for art education.

NAEA's mission is to advance art education through professional development, service, advancement of knowledge, and leadership.

Membership includes elementary and secondary art teachers, (and middle and senior high students in the National Art Honor Society programs) artists, administrators, museum educators, arts council staff, university professors, and students from throughout the United States and several foreign countries. It also includes publishers, manufacturers and suppliers of art materials, parents, students, retired art educators, and others concerned about quality art education in our schools.

The Association publishes *Art Education* journal, *Studies in Art Education*, and other professional papers on art education; holds an annual convention; conducts research; sponsors a teacher awards program; develops standards on student learning, school programs and teacher preparation; and co-sponsors workshops, seminars, and institutes on art education. For further information, visit our website at www.naea-reston.org.

1916 Association Drive
Reston, VA 20191

To order a copy of this book or obtain additional information, contact the National Art Education Association: www.naea-reston.org or 800-299-8321.

Design: Collaborative Communications Group, Washington, DC

Order No. 297

ISBN 978-1-890160-37-1

Dedication

Kathy would like to dedicate this book to her children, Windsor and Caribbea, and to her supportive husband, Jim. All three have always been a well-spring of inspiration.

Ruslan would like to dedicate this book to his wife, Mindy, and his children, Jordan and Jacob. Ruslan would also like to thank his parents, Nina and Aron, for their continuous unconditional support.

Acknowledgments

The authors wish to express their appreciation to those who helped us prepare this book. We would like to thank Sheila Torio for inspiring us to write this book and for her assistance in gathering information for the literature review. We would like to thank Phoebe Samuel for assisting us with the photographs, tables, and references as well as editing. A special thank you to Amy Bork for the use of her children's artwork.

Preface

Our book, *The Impact of Early Art Experiences on Literacy Development*, shows art and early childhood educators that simple art experiences can provide a wonderful venue to nurture literacy development. Being literate in the arts gives young children an advantage in learning to read and write. Experiences in studying lines, shapes, and colors can heighten awareness, facilitate word comprehension, and foster the development of reading and writing skills. When engaging in a variety of art experiences, young children can be trained to be observant and to look for details. They will develop visual discrimination skills that are crucial for reading and writing. Quality art experiences can also expand vocabulary and comprehension skills, while enriching critical thinking skills.

As Elliot Eisner (1988) notes, possessing a broad spectrum of literacy skills amplifies knowledge and understanding. Many of these skills are developed by creating, viewing, and discussing the visual arts.

This book includes a review of the literature on the importance of art experiences in facilitating the literacy process. We describe developmentally appropriate arts experiences that enhance literacy development from infancy to the third grade.

Significance of the Work

Young children begin the path to literacy by decoding symbols. The child learns how to manipulate symbols of the alphabet to understand written text. Becoming literate requires children to be observant, distinguish sounds, and look for details. The process also sharpens critical thinking and visual perception skills. Art experiences can play an important role in nurturing these skills.

The International Reading Association (IRA) and the National Association for the Education of Young Children (NAEYC) endorse the view that art experiences enhance literacy development, suggesting that adults should "provide opportunities for children to draw and print, using markers, crayons and pencils" (Neuman, Copple, Bredekamp, 2000, p. 20). Sigel (1984) invites us to broaden our school-based conceptions of meaning making to include forms like music, art, and drama—not just written language.

Data from the United States Department of Education indicates that students who are involved in the arts score higher on standardized tests (Catterall, 1998). Cooper-Solomon (1995) says that students would have greater academic abilities if at least 25% of school curriculum was devoted to the arts. April (2001) adds that "the arts do indeed increase students' achievement when achievement is conceived in rich and complex ways—authentic connections between the arts and the rest of learning" (p. 26). Further, "when well taught, the arts provide young people with authentic learning experiences that engage their minds, hearts, and bodies. The learning experiences are real and meaningful for them" (Fiske, 1999, p. ix).

Richards (1988) reminds us that the arts are the heart and soul of high-quality learning experiences, particularly in reading. Indeed, art experiences can serve as a bridge to literacy. Young children's artmaking is a nonverbal language, a system of symbols that emerge from early scribbling (Steele, 1998). "Putting ideas into the form of graphic representation allows the children to understand that their actions can communicate. This is an extraordinary discovery for young children because it helps them to realize that in order to communicate, there is a tool of communication much simpler than words" (Malaguzzi, 1998, p. 92). This simplicity entices children to begin the process of literacy development.

We must rethink the way we engage young children in early literacy learning. We can start by looking closely at the impact that art can have on helping children develop appropriate literacy experiences. We also must rethink what we mean by literacy. Is literacy solely the skill to read and write—or is it more complex than that? Should children be considered literate if they can draw their thinking on paper? Is drawing another way for children to construct knowledge, a way that can serve as a precursor to more traditional literacy experiences?

Art rooms are special workplaces. They are theaters for thinking both out loud and silently, for collaboration, celebration, and nurturance of children as they develop higher levels of cognition by engaging in hypothesizing, evaluating, and revisiting.

This book is unique in that it approaches literacy from an alternative perspective, thus providing a viewpoint that is different from traditional teacher resources on literacy. We believe that young children learn best through the rich and varied multisensory experiences that art provides.

Contents

1. The Role of the Visual Arts in Literacy Development

- Literacy learning in the United States — 1
- Why the visual arts are important in nurturing literacy — 3
- Artmaking as a naturally developing process — 5
- Literacy opportunities through viewing visual imagery — 6
- Literacy acquired through deciphering symbols in artworks — 8
- The visual arts as a developmentally appropriate literacy experience — 9

2. Fostering Literacy Through Early Visual Art Experiences

- The importance of scribbling — 11
- Developmental theories — 12
- Criticism of developmental theories — 13
- **The Irregular Scribbler** — 14
- Art experiences for the irregular scribbler — 15
- Aesthetic curiosity of the irregular scribbler — 16
- How adults can facilitate growth during the irregular scribbler phase — 16
- Aesthetic experiences for the irregular scribbler — 16
- **The Organized Scribbler** — 16
- Characteristics of children during the organized scribbler phase — 17
- Art experiences for the organized scribbler phase — 17
- How adults can facilitate learning during the organized scribbler phase — 18
- Aesthetic characteristics of children in the organized scribbler phase — 18
- Art appreciation and criticism games for the organized scribbler phase — 18
- Step-by-step art experiences for the organized scribbler — 19
- Step-by-step art appreciation games for the organized scribbler — 26
- **The Story Scribbler** — 28
- Additional characteristics of the story scribbler — 29
- Art experiences for the story scribbler phase — 29
- How adults can facilitate growth during the story scribbler phase — 29
- Aesthetic characteristics of children in the story scribbler phase — 29
- Step-by-step art experiences for the story scribbler — 30
- Step-by-step art appreciation games for the story scribbler — 41
- Summary — 44

3. Graphic Imagery That Begins to Convey Meaning

- Characteristics of children who draw to convey meaning — 47
- The literacy connection — 48
- Suggested art experiences — 49
- Aesthetic abilities — 49
- Art appreciation and criticism games for children in this phase — 49
- Step-by-step art experiences to convey meaning — 50
- Step-by-step art appreciation games to convey meaning — 72

4. Detailed Symbols As Meaning Makers

- Characteristics of children who draw as meaning makers — 79
- Literacy experiences during this phase — 80
- Art experiences for this phase — 80
- Aesthetic preferences of children during this phase — 80
- Step-by-step art experiences for children in this phase — 81
- Step-by-step art appreciation games for children in this phase — 91
- Summary — 94

5. Celebrating Children's Art and Literacy Experiences: Final Thoughts and Connections

- The art and literacy connection revisited — 97
- Displaying children's artworks — 99
- Reflecting and revisiting — 99
- Talking about art — 100
- Art auctions — 100
- Making art accessible today — 100

Book References — 103

Appendix A — 106
Mid-continent Research for Education and Learning

List of Benchmarks for Language Arts

Appendix B — 111
National Visual Art Standards

Appendix C — 112
Children's Books and Art Resources

About the Authors — 114

The Role of the Visual Arts in Literacy Development

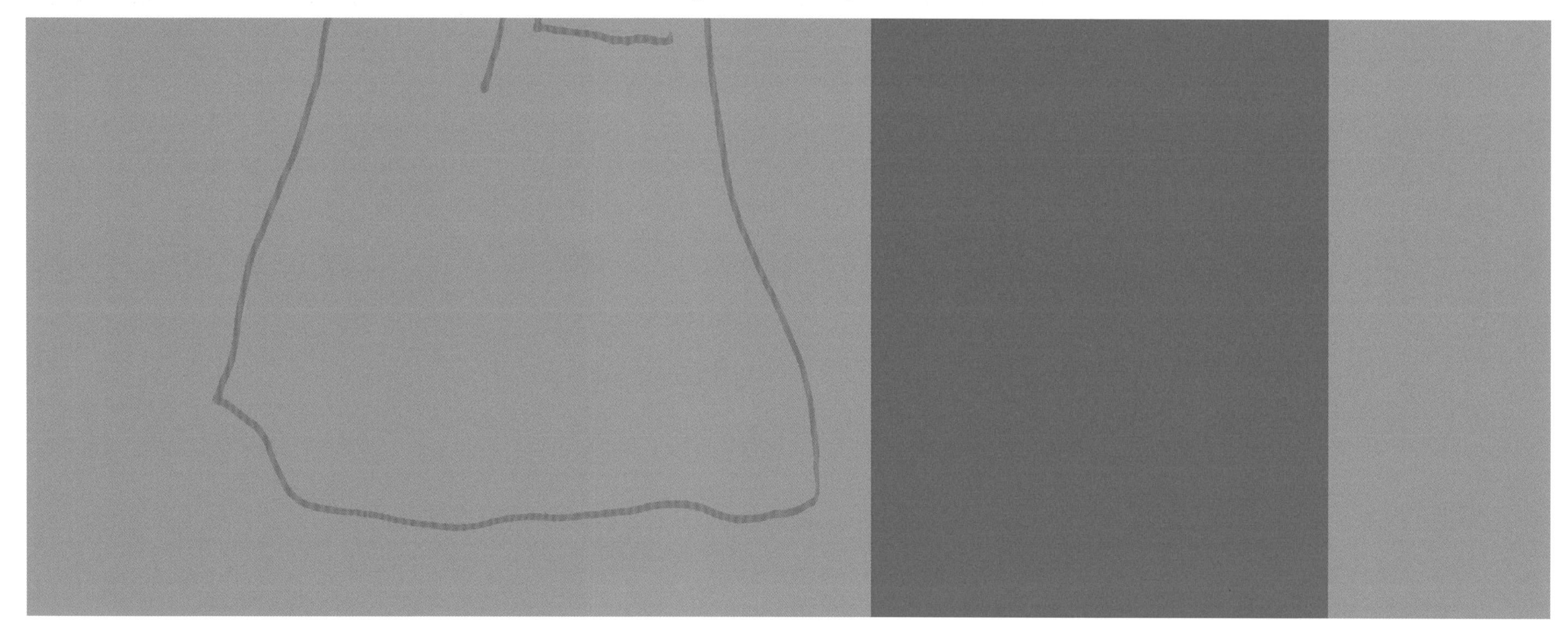

Literacy Learning in the United States

Low levels of literacy are endemic. According to the 2003 National Assessment of Adult Literacy (conducted by the National Center for Education Statistics), in the United States, 14% of the current population is below basic literacy skills level, while an additional 29% are just at the minimal basic level. This study clearly shows that close to half of all American adults have only very basic or below basic literacy skills.

Based on the data above, it should be of no surprise to anyone living in the United States why literacy is a top educational priority. According to the National Assessment of Educational Progress (NAEP), only 32% of 4th grade students are reading at or above their grade level. The NAEP also found that those students with higher performance scores on standardized tests continued to make progress, while low-achieving students scored lower than in previous years (NAEP, 2001). This trend poses a real literacy problem.

A child who has not yet learned to read . . . has no real opportunity to proceed through subsequent levels of the curriculum that depend on reading. Such a child has merely a bare opportunity to further his or her education, an opportunity in name only. (Howe, 1997, p. 3)

In the United States, the current expectation is for all children to function beyond minimum standards of literacy.

Today the definition of basic proficiency in literacy calls for a fairly high standard of reading comprehension and analysis. The main reason is that literacy requirements of most jobs have increased significantly and are expected to increase further in the future. (Neuman, Copple, Bredekamp, 2000, p. 4)

The infusion of technology in the workplace and home has itself become a form of literacy as children and adults must master this new language to be successful. Language can no longer be viewed as being only oral and written. Understanding this new digital language is becoming critical to the achievement of today's children.

A child who has not yet learned to read . . . has no real opportunity to proceed through subsequent levels of the curriculum that depend on reading.

(Howe, 1997)

Literacy can be broadly defined as the ability to read and write proficiently. "But more and more, the texts that students are being asked to understand and interpret are not simply words; they are words and pictures" (Wachowiak & Clements, 2006, p. 74). Therefore, traditional literacy learning is no longer enough. Eisner (2002) notes that:

Language is often a very limited vehicle for the description of qualities. . . . The assumption that language will always serve as an adequate means for describing what students are to be able to do and know is itself problematic. (p. 165)

Failure to nurture young children during early literacy experiences may limit their reading and writing proficiency later in life.

We are bombarded with images in the popular media, such as billboards, Internet advertisers, magazine covers, package designs, and television. To decipher these images, we need to broaden our definition of literacy to include *visual literacy*, which is "the ability to analyze and interpret visual images" (Wachowiak & Clements, 2006, p. 74). This type of literacy, which has not been given enough attention in today's culture, needs to be carefully considered. Visual literacy differs from traditional literacy in that it requires one to evoke meaning from visual images as opposed to the written word. It is clear that a pedagogical shift must take place in our homes and schools if we are to meet the literacy needs of today's young learners. This requires thinking "out of the box" and coming up with new ways to deal with an old problem. To build a solid foundation, effective literacy experiences need to be provided as early as possible:

Even in the first few months of life, children begin to experiment with language. Young babies make sounds that imitate the tones and rhythms of adult talk; they "read" gestures and facial expressions, and they begin to associate sound sequences frequently heard—spoken words—with their referents. (Neuman, Copple, Bredekamp, 2000, p. 6)

Failure to nurture young children during these early literacy experiences may limit their reading and writing proficiency later in life.

What does a literacy experience for young children consist of? It involves the decoding of symbols and learning how to manipulate alphabet symbols to understand written text. Literacy also requires children to be observant, distinguish sounds, look for details, and sharpen their critical thinking and visual discrimination skills. This is where visual art experiences can play an important role in nurturing literacy skills.

The International Reading Association (IRA) and the National Association for the Education of Young Children (NAEYC) endorse the importance of art experiences in literacy development, suggesting that parents should "provide opportunities for children to draw and print, using markers, crayons and pencils" (Neuman, Copple, Bredekamp, 2000, p. 20). This is not a revelation. In the 19th century, Friederich Froebel, the founder of kindergarten, saw the important connection between drawing and writing. He described it as a seamless relationship: "The word and the drawing, therefore, belong together inseparable, as light and shadow, night and day, soul and body do" (1974, originally published 1826).

Today, researchers such as Wachowiak and Clements (2006), Clay (1995), Eisner (2002), and Anning (1997) invite us to consider broadening our school-based conceptions of meaning making to include the visual arts.

Picture 1.1: Picture Word

Why the Visual Arts Are Important in Nurturing Literacy

"For all children, at all ability levels, the arts play a central role in cognitive, motor, language, and social-emotional development. The arts motivate and engage children in learning, stimulate memory and facilitate understanding, enhance symbolic communication, promote relationships, and provide an avenue for building competence. The arts are natural for young children." (Goldhawk, 1998, p. v)

More specifically, the visual arts play a major role in literacy development of young children. Drawing, especially, is important.

Drawing precedes writing and is an important element in the "prehistory" of children's writing, just as hieroglyphic pictograms probably preceded written alphabets, and drawing continues to be a valuable supplement and complement to written language in more sophisticated communication. (Wachowiak & Clements 2006, p. 67)

Drawing is a way that young children can communicate their ideas, especially if they have a limited verbal vocabulary. These drawings can enable children to construct knowledge and convey meaning through visual images.

Richards (1988) reminds us that the visual arts are the heart and soul of high-quality learning experiences, particularly in reading. With that in mind, appropriate art experiences can serve as a bridge to literacy for young children. As parents and educators, we must keep in mind that artmaking is an important nonverbal language, made up of a system of symbols emerging from children's early scribbling experiences (Steele, 1998).

Putting ideas into the form of graphic representation allows the children to understand that their actions can communicate. This is an extraordinary discovery for young children because it helps them to realize that in order to communicate, there is a tool of communication much simpler than words. (Malaguzzi, 1998, p. 92)

Children need this simplicity to spark an interest in literacy exploration and engagement. Graphic representation (that is, drawing and painting) can serve as a stepping stone to more formal literacy experiences.

Making art draws on . . . (various) ways of learning, most immediately through the acts of organizing, reflecting, judging, discriminating, selecting, and representing the raw material of the world. These thought functions are crucial to constructing meaning in every area of learning. (Engel, 2002, p. 4)

These skills are imperative during the literacy acquisition process. Teachers and parents should use this time to expose children to as many of these learning tasks as possible.

Research with younger children suggests that those who are encouraged to draw and scribble stories at an early age will later learn to compose stories more easily, more effectively, and with greater confidence than children who do not have this type of encouragement (Applebee, 1978; Clay, 1995). Creating imagery using symbolic language and thinking metaphorically are skills for future quality writing. For example, children use mental images to construct stories. The child doesn't visualize words in this process, but rather images that are used in traditional writing and storytelling. Wachowiak and Clements (2006) note that:

> *Even after we learn to write, drawing is essential, for we learn through representation. We construct meaning by formulating our own representations. While these representations are usually verbal or written, they may also be diagrammatic or pictorial. (p. 67)*

The visual imagery that children experience through their artmaking serves as a stimulus for future creative writing. All children begin to draw before they can write. But as they get older, their artwork naturally begins to include more traditional forms of literacy, such as letters, words, and numbers, to further tell the story.

> *The interplay of the two forms of communication is a powerful motivator for both drawing and writing. Both the artwork and the written passages offer representations of the same cluster of things—each provides a window into the child's world. (Wachowiak & Clements, 2006, p. 67)*

In their own picture making, children will naturally construct visual patterns that will later be implemented in formal writing.

Barrs (1988) also sees art as an important part of the writing process for young children who continuously fluctuate between the two forms of communication. As children develop in their picture making, from scribbles to more recognizable symbols, they naturally come to a point where the adult observer is not sure if the graphic rendering is a word or a picture. In their own picture making, children will naturally construct visual patterns that will later be implemented in formal writing. Eventually, "children begin to turn scribbling into drawing and to separate writing from both" (Anning, 1997, p. 225). Therefore, visual art experiences should be encouraged in order to nurture this natural process toward literacy. Drawing, as Engel (2002) suggests, is "a natural symbol-making activity, is a path to knowing, a means of learning" (p. 20) and a direct connection to formal literacy experiences.

Another perspective is provided by Olshansky (1995) who suggests that "the process of image finding" is central to the prewriting phase (p. 45). Her research suggests that the addition of the "artmaking" component to the writing process nurtures imagination, more fully developed story plots, the use of more descriptive language, and the sequencing of stories with a beginning, middle, and end.

To exclude visual art experiences from early childhood education would inhibit children from experiencing the world from a variety of perspectives. By supporting the art experiences of young children, we are providing them with opportunities to manipulate a variety of media to illustrate their understanding of concepts and ideas.

> *Children are forever reminded to "use words" to express a range of emotions and needs. Introducing the visual arts into their daily lives gives children another appropriate and satisfying means of expression. It is as though we are saying to them "use the arts"—speak with images and gestures. (Epstein & Trimis, 2002, p. 25)*

Artmaking as a Naturally Developing Process

Artmaking is a process that begins at birth. Infants use their fingers and arms to "air scribble" for kinesthetic pleasure. This experience can be viewed as a precursor to later scribbling that they will perform with paper and various drawing tools. All children gravitate toward artmaking. It is a natural process that children use to express themselves. In fact, children who lack verbal skills use art as a vehicle to share their thoughts and ideas with others. For many young nonverbal children, art is perhaps their only source to relay how they are feeling or what they are thinking.

When children scribble, their physical and mental gestures become visible. The marks of their bodies and minds take on permanence. Scribbles prepare infant brains to record the sound of speech, the sounds of music, quantities and relationships and ideas—things we cannot touch and we cannot see. Their brains are learning to make the invisible world visible. When your baby is hungry for food, you feed your baby. When your baby is hungry for art and literacy, feed your baby with marks. (Sheridan, 2002)

According to Gardner's theory of multiple intelligences, some children prefer to engage in artmaking experiences as a means to convey their knowledge or, at times, as a way to think through complex issues (Gardner, 1983).

> ***Scribbles prepare infant brains to record the sound of speech, the sounds of music, quantities and relationships and ideas—things we cannot touch and we cannot see.***
>
> ***(Sheridan, 2002)***

Children's early scribbling attempts nurture early skill development. Motor development, visual discrimination, cognition, creativity, social skills, and recognition of cause and effect are enhanced through scribbling experiences. Motor development is improved through the use of different sizes and types of tools. Through this exploratory process, children learn how to use these tools effectively and hold them in ways that promote skills that are important for future writing. Children use visual discrimination when they differentiate one type of line from another—for example, a curvy line versus a straight line. Cognition is affected when children construct symbols by using various media. Constructing symbols helps children understand concepts they are trying to convey. The process of making art allows children to think in different ways and challenges them to represent symbolically what they experience in the real world. The arts not only inform our construction of meaning, but they also expand our understanding of the world (Eisner, 1991).

Creativity is enhanced as children are given free rein to explore the "100 languages" (discussed later in this chapter) in multiple ways. Socially, artmaking helps children share their ideas, via symbol systems, through conversations that take place during these art experiences. This process builds vocabulary necessary for traditional language development. Children learn about cause and effect by realizing that various tools leave different marks. For example, using a thick paintbrush will leave a different mark than a thin paintbrush. Therefore, providing choices of materials is important for the child.

> ***The teacher should put careful thought into the selection of materials provided for the child. These materials will influence the thinking process of the child and the manner in which they produce their artistic creations. These graphic visual images, unlike speech, stick; they remain visible and can be worked upon. One can inspect them; one can make alterations and then make comparisons among the alterations made. (Eisner, 2002, p. 114)***

Artmaking allows children to reconstruct their experiences by using various media to create symbols—thereby helping children understand the world.

> ***Objects and events of the world are known through many sensory modalities, and each contributes to children's awareness of the features of the object to be drawn. It is this awareness that manifests itself in children's graphic representations. (Eisner, 2002, p. 113)***

Children's art helps adults see that children understand the world, but more importantly *how* they understand it. The symbols children use to represent their understanding become increasingly complex, illustrating the child's ability to think in more abstract ways. This complexity and attention to detail in their artmaking also increases as children have more opportunities to explore various art media.

Literacy Opportunities Through Viewing Visual Imagery

Using Artworks to Encourage Language Aquisition

Drawing and literacy are strongly connected, but there are other ways that the visual arts can be used to nurture literacy. Because children learn language through social interaction, it is important to provide opportunities for all children to talk about art (Newton, 1995).

Rich literacy opportunities are available to young children not only as they draw, but also as they look at art. In our visual society we are constantly striving to derive meaning from the various visual images we encounter daily. For many, this can be an overwhelming process because art is such a unique language system. Viewing art and talking about it involves a decoding of symbols in order to decipher meaning (Eisner, 1976). This process involves the ability to perceptually separate figure from ground. It also involves using one's ability to recognize and decipher messages and information conveyed by visual images, while also understanding how images affect the viewer. These skills are important, especially when one becomes engaged in traditional reading experiences.

The process of viewing art in order to derive meaning is art criticism, which includes *description, analysis, interpretation,* and *judgment* (Feldman, 1985). *Description* is the process of taking inventory of elements such as line, color, shape, and texture. Here, one describes or at least pays attention to what one sees in a work of art. *Analysis* goes a step farther. It involves looking at the elements of design, such as line, shape, color, and texture, and the way they interconnect through the principles of design such as balance or focal point. *Interpretation* allows the viewer to determine the meaning of a work. What is the artist trying to say? *Judgment* is deciding on the degree of artistic and aesthetic merit. In other words, does the viewer like the work? Why or why not? All of these components are necessary for a quality experience in art criticism. We naturally go through this process whether or not we are aware of it. Some theorists suggest ways of looking at art through non-Western lenses (McFee & Degge, 1980; Lanier, 1982; Chapman, 1978). But, for the sake of simplicity, we will use the Feldman model despite its shortcomings. Seasoned consumers of art will have a more in-depth experience than novice viewers who may need guidance along the way.

Art criticism and appreciation might seem too sophisticated for early childhood audiences, but young children can participate. Engaging children in this process will allow them to question and interpret what they see; weigh evidence and information; examine their own reactions; and increase their perceptual awareness. Needless to say, all of these can nurture literacy development.

Research by Douglas, Schwartz, and Taylor (1981) suggests that attention given to images and image characteristics that are evocative for learners and are developmentally appropriate may result in a more meaningful learning experience. Using art images in the classroom or visiting museums offer opportunities for important reflection and expression of language skills.

Genishi and Dyson (1984) recommend collaborative talk to facilitate verbalization and language development. When children view an artwork, they can exchange ideas and learn new vocabulary and word meanings.

By discussing artworks, children learn that visual symbols can communicate ideas (Cole & Schaefer, 1990), but that these ideas can also be interpreted in many ways depending on each child's experiences. Children learn that just because they interpret a piece of art in a certain way does not mean that others will view it similarly. Teachers can serve as role models for young children by using rich oral language to describe qualities in the artwork being viewed, and by providing their own interpretations. This process will help young children with acquiring and developing language and understanding that different interpretations are possible.

According to Cole (1994), ways to engage children in responding to an artwork include *play*, *conversations*, and *authenticating the experience*. *Play* involves finding connections between the artwork and the viewer by using tangible objects. *Conversations* engage the child in talking about the artwork and focusing on details. *Authenticating the experience* guides children into a related studio experience (that is, a hands-on art project).

Some examples of using these strategies when viewing artworks to facilitate language and literacy development are:

- simple games, such as inventing stories about the characters or scenes portrayed in a painting or a sculpture;
- looking for objects in the artwork that begin with each letter of the alphabet;
- thinking of words that describe emotions conveyed in a portrait.

All of these are examples of both *play* and *conversation*.

Another way to use artworks is providing compare-and-contrast opportunities. For example, children can be encouraged to compare two artworks with opposite qualities. This strategy works well because it is often easier for young children to discern differences rather than similarities (Newton, 1995). An example of *conversation*, this exercise gives children a wonderful opportunity to use rich language to describe artworks and provides them a chance "to look, think, understand, and learn" (Eglinton, 2003, p. 7).

When children view an artwork, they can exchange ideas and learn new vocabulary and word meanings.

As children get older, works of art can also serve as the impetus for creative writing and storytelling. The teacher may begin to tell a story and then point to a child to continue telling the story or continue the story through a graphic representation. The process goes on until all children have had a chance to participate. Such an opportunity can:

> ***provide encounters that foster the capacity to construct interpretations. The need to interpret is necessary in life, since reliable knowledge is often unavailable or filled with ambiguous and conflicting data. The interpretation of works of art not only enables one to construct understandings about them, but enables individuals to interpret other situations where life's circumstances are uncertain or unclear. (Efland, 2002, p. 161)***

If artworks from a museum are not readily available, more accessible works of art can be found in the popular media—picture books, postcards, calendars, or museum websites.

In a picture book, the pictures and the accompanying words work together to create a meaningful experience for the reader. In essence, pictures do have meaning and are an important component in literacy acquisition because they can influence reading skills (Lewis, 2001). In fact, "reading pictures is a gateway to letter and word recognition" (Epstein & Trimis, 2002, p. 36).

Literacy Acquired Through Deciphering Symbols in Artworks

Artworks provide frames for reading the world. These frames, theories, concepts, images, and narratives parse the world in particular ways. Becoming socialized within a culture means acquiring these frames, for they allow you to join and participate in a discourse community, where discourse refers to the sharing of any form in which meaning is encoded and can be decoded. Common frames make a shared way of life possible. (Eisner, 2002, p. 85)

Eisner is saying that each culture communicates within its own world of symbols, not only in the written word, but also in the visual arts. Being able to decipher symbols used in the written word is only a part of being literate. The ability to decode symbols in the visual arts reflects an understanding of the essence of a culture and its history—an important component that makes us thoroughly literate.

Newborns begin immediately to make sense of symbols, colors, shapes, and images they encounter. As children get older, they begin to understand that culture defines how we view and interpret symbols. For example, American children learn very early to associate the color blue with males and pink with females. Extending this decoding of symbols while using artwork can nurture this "reading" process. By looking at artworks and participating in adult-child discourse, children learn the meanings of symbols and how those symbols function in their culture.

Picture 1.2: Rusyn

Visual artists have their hands on the pulse of society. They reflect the undercurrents of social, political, and religious happenings via symbols used in their artwork. For example, the sun symbol, with points radiating from a center circle, is a prominent figure in Rusyn (a minority culture group in Eastern Europe) embroidery designs. Within this culture, the sun is the oldest symbol found in the visual arts and signifies life. In pre-Christian days it was a deity symbol. This same symbol can be found in a form of African textiles called Adinkra cloth. In this culture, however, this sun symbol signifies royalty. Unless one is visually literate, such symbols could not be decoded and read, thus the meaning of any work containing these symbols would be lost. Teaching children to decode such symbols can empower them to read and understand symbols prevalent in a culturally diverse world. By not exposing children to such opportunities, we are shortchanging them of valuable literacy lessons. Furthermore:

Art provides the material that enables the growth of a child's perceptual discernment. Looking at, reflecting upon, creating, and experiencing art teaches, guides, and refines perception. . . . True perception requires thought. (Eglinton, 2003, p. 7)

Picture 1.3: Adinkra Cloth

The Visual Arts as a Developmentally Appropriate Literacy Experience

Parents and teachers should not focus on reading and writing with preschoolers (unless the child shows interest) because it may lead to failure and disrupt future literacy experiences. Early inappropriate literacy experiences may frustrate the child, leading to withdrawal from subsequent literacy experiences.

A simple redefinition of literacy can help children experience literacy in appropriate ways. The Reggio Emilia approach uses the term "100 languages" (Edwards, Gandini & Forman, 1998) to mean that children have at their disposal 100 languages and many more to construct and communicate their knowledge. By redefining literacy in this manner, we no longer focus only on the oral or written cues; rather, we allow children the opportunity to use art materials (such as clay, wire, paint, markers, and crayons) to engage in alternative literacy experiences that are meaningful to them at their developmental level. Furthermore, these experiences do not frustrate children because they are using skills that they naturally possess, which helps nurture their emerging passion for continuous literacy development.

Adult intervention during this literacy process is crucial. While children develop graphic skills through a natural process (Kellogg, 1970), it is imperative that adults facilitate this process to help children accelerate their acquisition of literacy (Anning, 1997).

The following chapters will discuss the nurturing of traditional and visual literacy skills through art experiences in these ways: making art, looking at art, and talking about art.

Fostering Literacy Through Early Visual Art Experiences

The Importance of Scribbling

Traditionally, adults have dismissed the artwork of young children. In many educational settings, children have been conditioned to undervalue their aesthetic choices and artistic abilities, and to view scribbling as a waste of time. *Scribbling* has become a term adults use when they cannot describe or understand the art of the young child. Children, however, innately enjoy spontaneously moving a finger or drawing tool over a surface and leaving a record of this kinesthetic exercise. Although the construction of markings during scribbling makes little sense to adults, it is a valuable exercise because it sets the stage for future formal writing activities. For children in any culture to develop as writers, they need time to kinesthetically experience scribbling, which builds the foundation to form lines associated with letter formation.

Cognitive capabilities in children develop through the impact of their own scribbles.

At an age far earlier than once assumed, children begin to use marks, lines, and shapes to stand for something. It might be a person or object or a mark might represent movement, action, or the sound of an object as well. Meaning making (or meaning finding) is a remarkable development; often uncelebrated because it can be difficult to detect. As many young toddlers remain silent or don't utter words that we understand, we simply don't know when they begin to use marks to stand for something. (Kolbe, 2005, p. 10)

Children's basic scribbles permit a detailed and comprehensive description of the work of young children (Kellogg, 1970).

A common adult mistake is to prevent the child from scribbling. Adults who do not nurture children's scribbling and instead encourage copy work or the use of coloring books are not acting in the best interest of the child. Children need scribbling opportunities to develop their cognitive functioning as well as fine and gross motor skills. Visual discrimination, a skill necessary for both reading and writing, is also being developed during the scribbling process.

Young children need to feel that the adult viewer accepts their work. For young children, growth in art is a delicate matter that must be nurtured and respected. Sharing in a child's art activity can give the adult a better understanding of the child's process. According to Bland (1957):

Adults will help the child best if they understand what he/she is trying to do. Understanding underlies respect and this goes deeper than mere cordial acceptance. The child needs respect in order to go forward with the confidence in what he/she has to say and in his/her mastery of the means to say it. (p. 37)

It is fundamental to children's growth in art to provide them with time to explore what they paint, model, or construct. Perhaps the finished product will not meet adult standards, but to the child, the finished product is unimportant. Children value the sheer enjoyment of changing what they

Adults who do not nurture children's scribbling and instead encourage copy work or the use of coloring books are not acting in the best interest of the child.

are making and the process of discovery. According to Clay (1995), children love to play with pencils and pens. For them, these tools allow for new discoveries in mark making. These types of activities are very satisfying for young children and development seems to have more to do with opportunity to explore mark making than the actual intelligence or age of the child. When scribbling, children want to express their reactions to certain stimuli, thus the guidance they receive should be subtle, skillful, well-timed, and conducive to creative expression. However, research indicates that teachers don't spend much time interacting with children when they are involved in the artmaking process (Tizard, Blatchford, Burke, Farguar & Plewis, 1988; Mortimore, Sammons, Stoll, Lewis & Ecob, 1988; Alexander, 1992). Teachers need to become educated in how to appropriately intervene.

> ***...In educational contexts where children's drawing intentions are valued and their graphicacy is nurtured by instruction and supported by feedback from adults, drawing offers children a powerful tool for making sense of the world.*** *(Anning, 1997, p. 227)*

It's important to understand the path that children take in the evolution of scribbling. Below we discuss the phases of scribbling to help adults appreciate the importance of these stages and how to best support children's experiences and the learning process.

First, though, we will discuss developmental theories and their criticisms.

Developmental Theories

Developmental theories can provide insights about children's attempts at graphics and ways teachers and other adults can appropriately motivate and instruct. There are various developmental theories about children's graphic development. Several of these theories will be described here. One view describes the process of unfolding, where the child is permitted to naturally evolve, as graphic abilities are believed to be innate (Kellogg, 1970). The teacher's role in this approach is one of nurturing and providing an environment that is conducive and not restrictive to growth. The other approach is more directive (Braswell & Callanan, 2003). The directive approach supports the notion that if children are left to discover on their own, they will be unable to reach their full potential in art and literacy. The teacher must guide this growth process. Gardner and Winner (1976) suggest that the natural unfolding process seems to occur at the earlier stages of life, but as children get older, they become more influenced by their environment and require more facilitation of the growth process by a knowledgeable adult. Thus, it is okay to let young children engage in a natural unfolding process, but then begin to add more direction as they get older and their skill improves.

Kellogg (1970) supports the "natural unfolding" process. She believes that children's drawings are independent of their observations of the environment. Instead, their drawings stem from an intrinsic evolution of scribbles and shapes. Drawings are not representations of real objects, but are combinations of symbols previously made (Anning, 1997). Art is self-taught, as children achieve various stages simply by engaging in their own activities. Kellogg (1970) further claims that the child tends to become confused when presented with adult standards to imitate, as it is visually illogical to the child's system of self-taught art symbols. Children will learn by teaching themselves with little or no adult intervention.

Eisner (1972) offers yet another view. He believes children's art development results from their experiences and learning.

Indeed, there seems to be a natural, evolving process at work when children scribble. But, because children do not live in a vacuum, there will be influences on this process. Children learn from other children and are great imitators. Adults should be mindful of such views and be able to intervene in this process when necessary. For example, adults can talk about the kinds of lines and shapes they see in children's scribbles, or they can talk about how the drawing tool is held by the child to achieve a certain quality of line marking. Understanding the importance of scribbles and marks on paper can provide teachers and parents with much needed insight about their role as facilitator during this growth process.

Criticism of Developmental Theories

Theories about developmental stages have been criticized in the last several decades (Wilson & Wilson, 1981; Kindler, 1997). One of the charges is that stage theories fail to take into account the influences of culture on development. Norms or averages used in stage theories often do not apply in non-Western cultures. Critics of stage theories claim that because of the vast amount of stimulation from the mass media it is unrealistic to assume that a modern child develops in a vacuum. According to Kindler (1997):

> ***A linear conception of growth focuses attention on one category of pictorial production, and manifestations of pictorial activity outside its boundaries are not addressed within the framework of stage theories. (p. 18)***

Wilson and Wilson (1981) further contend that children are influenced by the media in their culture as well as by other children and adults. Thus, what they see and can imitate becomes a powerful vehicle in their drawing development. Kindler (1997) adds another criticism:

> ***Optical realism is not a cross-culturally preferred representational convention and, as art history demonstrates, it is not a consistent goal even within the boundaries of Western cultural tradition. ... Thus, realism-centered stage theories seem to use an irrelevant baseline for considerations of artistic growth. (p. 18)***

Failure to allow for individual differences as children progress differently through the stages is another criticism. Another limitation is the focus on drawing. Stage theories exclude other modes of self-expression in the visual arts, such as sculpture.

With such shortcomings, why should developmental stages be considered? Although there are inherent problems, these studies offer information that can be valuable to teachers and parents. Lewis (1982) suggests: "The details of development vary. The essential course of development remains the same. We need not dispose of knowledge we have. We need to build on it" (p. 8). Developmental theories can provide teachers and parents with insights about the graphical attempts of children and how to best motivate and instruct them (Hurwitz & Day, 1991).

We align ourselves with Kindler (1997), whose model is "grounded in the assumption that artistic development is a phenomenon which occurs in an interactive social environment and that artistic learning involves a social component" (p. 20). With this in mind, we will stress in the following chapters that artistic development (not confining ourselves to only pictorial) occurs in the socio-cultural milieu. Every child is different, with various experiences and influences. These factors greatly influence the artistic process. It is important for the adult, while facilitating the learning process, to refrain from engaging in value judgments.

The artistic process, as discussed in this book, is a semiotic evolution (the development and construction of symbols from simplest to more complex). It is how meaning is constructed and understood through the use of individual and groups of symbols. This process not only includes mark making, but also constructing with various three-dimensional materials, using body movements, and making sounds. It is imperative that adults become "co-explorers" with the child during this important learning process.

Literacy, regardless of socio-cultural setting, is basically a process of decoding symbols. This process is heavily influenced by the socio-cultural milieu.

> ***Within a general process of development, two qualitatively different lines of development, differing in origin, can be distinguished: the elementary processes, which are of biological origin, on the one hand, and the higher psychological functions, of sociocultural origin, on the other. The history of child behavior is born from the interweaving of these two lines. (Vygotsky, 1978, p. 46)***

Taking into consideration Vygotsky's "zone of proximal development" (a child's range of ability with and without assistance from a teacher) is important in evaluating the artistic learning process, which includes making and viewing works of art. As we discuss each artistic phase, we will recommend how adults can facilitate the learning process. We will explore various artistic processes, not just drawing.

Kindler (1997) says, "much of children's production cross[es] the boundaries of a single medium and embrace[s] visual, vocal, and gestural elements in the creation of a piece" (p. 22). We will take a holistic view of children's psychological and brain development, and their physical development and milestones. We will look at instances where there is change in semiotic activity. Bear in mind that these are not stages, but provide a range of behaviors in an attempt to avoid any socio-cultural biases.

The Irregular Scribbler

The phases as described below and throughout the rest of this book come from a combination of theorists including: Kellogg (1970), Lowenfeld & Brittain (1987), and Gardner (1980).

One of the goals of this book is to move away from assigning ages to particular phases as not all children reach each phase at the same time. Our goal is for parents and teachers to learn how to take cues from children as opposed to being driven by a child's age. The phases presented below flow into one another. The age of the child may not necessarily dictate the phase the child may actually be in, what is more of a factor is the child's actual experiences with the visual arts.

The child in the "irregular scribbler" phase engages in a perceptual and motor adjustment to the world. The child does no drawing or visual symbolic manipulation. However, these children will go through the motions of scribbling as they flail their arms in the air—"air scribbles." Later, the child can coordinate vision and grasping, but is unable to construct conceptual images. As extensive perceptual activity continues and as visual and tactile movements become more coordinated, the child begins to develop mental images.

During this phase, the child is capable of imitating behavior. He or she makes unorganized attempts at symbolic representation in the form of scribbles. The child can make scribbles without looking at the paper. These random renderings vary in length and direction. The size of the child's motions recorded on paper relates to the child's size. The longer the child's reach, the longer the markings are made on the paper; the shorter the child's reach, the smaller the markings are on the paper.

The irregular scribbler phase includes basic scribbles where movements display a variety of muscular tension that does not require much hand-eye control. Scribbles made during this phase require eye control only for placing scribbles within a defined parameter. Often children will not look at the drawing surface as they scribble because they are focused on a distraction in the room.

Each scribble offers evidence of the child's perception and early evidence of controlled shaping. Early scribbles are not attempts at portraying the visual environment, but will evolve into shapes that are more recognizable. Below are additional characteristics of the random scribbler:

- Uses large muscles
- Makes scribbles for kinesthetic pleasure
- Uses whole-hand grip on the marking tool
- Makes random and haphazard markings on the drawing surface
- Makes "bang dots" (when the child hits the marking tool on the drawing surface)

Picture 2.1: Irregular Scribble

Children at this phase are unable to talk, but can make one-syllable babbling sounds. "There is no evidence that these vocal cues support the semiotic process" (Kindler, 1997, p. 26). They can respond to words or simple questions with a "yes" or "no." Other characteristics include the ability to sit up while attempting to pull themselves up to stand and to start to toddle. These children display an interest in pictures and can recognize themselves in a mirror (Allen & Marotz, 2007).

Art Experiences for the Irregular Scribbler

These children can engage in art experiences to develop skills in visual perception and discrimination, hand-eye coordination, problem solving, fine and gross motor skills, vocabulary, and sequencing, all of which are essential for future literacy experiences. For example, children need visual perception and discrimination to make various letter forms when writing and to differentiate words while reading. Hand-eye coordination is needed for writing skills. Problem solving will be used to decipher words as a child reads and writes; fine and gross motor skills are needed to properly hold a writing tool and write legibly. The acquiring of new vocabulary words helps the child become literate. Sequencing enables a child to read and follow the plot of a story. Children at this stage cannot do any of these activities, but the groundwork can be provided to nurture these skills.

There are many tools that young children can use for scribbling. Children will begin to realize that there is a relationship between their actions and the markings made on the drawing surface. They want to repeat certain actions. Offering the child a variety of surfaces to draw on and tools to use is essential at this time. Children who are provided with extensive experiences with graphic materials will, in later phases, begin to use letters in their artwork (Kellogg, 1970; Zepeda-de-Kane, 1980). Children in this phase can use the following materials.

Drawing and Painting Surfaces

Paper should be secured to the tray of the child's high chair using masking tape. Thus, children won't become frustrated because the paper moves while they are making their marks. Consider these materials and activities:

- Drawing on textured materials like sandpaper and corrugated cardboard
- Painting on sidewalks with water
- Drawing or painting on newspaper
- Making chalk drawings on the sidewalk
- Using papers cut into a variety of shapes and different lengths and widths
- Drawing on Mylar and other shiny surfaces
- Drawing on mirrors and acetate

A Variety of Tools to Use

- Crayon muffins (Break up old crayons, place pieces assorted by color in a muffin tin and melt at 200-250 degrees. When melted, remove from the oven to cool, then pop "muffins" out of the muffin tin.)
- Nontoxic markers (keep caps away from child) including Gel FX markers for drawing on slick surfaces such as mirrors, acetate, etc.
- Paintbrushes in assorted sizes

Safety Note: Children this age need adult supervision at all times. Children are still placing objects into their mouths, which poses a choking hazard.

A Sample Drawing Activity

Tape a corrugated cardboard piece to a high chair tray. Place a piece of paper on top and secure with tape. Using a crayon muffin, the child can explore graphic mark making over the textured surface. Textures can be changed as desired. Other textures might include sandpaper, a window screen, or bubble wrap. Packs of plastic textured sheets can also be purchased at a teacher supply or art supply store.

It is important for adults to interact with children during their explorations in scribbling. Make comments using descriptive vocabulary, such as, "Look at the squiggly lines you're making," as you point to those lines. Children will not fully comprehend what you are saying, but it is a beginning point for fostering literacy. Children's early mark-making attempts can be inhibited if their environment is not supportive (Hurwitz & Day, 1991). A nurturing adult is essential during this discovery process.

Children will begin to realize that there is a relationship between their actions and the markings made on the drawing surface.

Aesthetic Curiosity of the Irregular Scribbler

Children in the irregular scribbler phase have aesthetic preferences. Research in developmental psychology suggests that young children are more capable of appreciating art then they are typically given credit for (Epstein, 2001). In fact, Schirrmacher (1998) found that "aesthetics and young children go hand in hand. Babies begin by exploring and marveling at their world. Over time, children internalize adult 'don'ts' and learn not to look, listen, touch, taste, or smell. They take their senses and the world of lines, shapes, colors, and design for granted" (p. 189). Adults should provide experiences that stimulate young children's aesthetic curiosity during this phase. Below are ways that adults can support young children's aesthetic development, while also nurturing literacy.

How Adults Can Facilitate Growth During the Irregular Scribble Phase

Attention and enthusiasm are the best encouragement during this time. Scribble along with the child on the same paper or a different one. Children should be encouraged to scribble as much as possible, whether scribbling in their food on the high chair tray or using art materials. Again, it is important for the adult to talk to the child as they share in art experiences. Siblings or peers can join in as well.

Aesthetic Experiences for the Irregular Scribbler

Although children at this stage are mostly nonverbal, it is important for adults to talk to the child while engaging in these activities and become a co-constructor of learning.

- Show the child brightly colored illustrations in children's books with multicultural and anti-bias pictures.
- Hang brightly colored or black-and-white mobiles 12 inches above the baby's head.
- Attach nonbreakable mirrors safely to the crib.
- Post visuals that are high contrast and in bright colors or black-and-white.
- Provide an assortment of crumpled paper, newspaper, corrugated cardboard.
- Provide tubs filled with water, shaved ice, pudding, or Jell-O for tactile stimulation.
- Provide brightly colored blocks for constructions.
- Look at a variety of art reproductions with the child. Include photographs of children.
- Show books and artworks that have clear pictures of familiar objects to best engage children at this stage.

The Organized Scribbler

Picture 2.2: Organized Scribble

Children in this phase can imitate behavior internally and externally. They begin to make a connection between their motions and their graphic markings on paper. These children have more visual control over their markings as they begin to discover relationships between their recordings on paper. Other characteristics of mark making during this stage include:

- Makes smaller marks with better control
- Repeats marking motions
- Begins use of wrist motion
- Stays within the drawing area
- Includes a variety of lines and loops in the scribbling
- Watches while scribbling

If given a new material to explore, such as clay, the child will poke, prod, and pound it with their fingers as they experience this new medium. "Rolling tiny coils is one of the first skills that children develop, followed by making tiny balls. Coils are easier to make than balls" (Kolbe, 1997, p. 8). An adult should supervise this experience, as the child might still tend to want to taste the materials.

When given collage materials, children marvel at the materials' sensory qualities. When gluing the materials to a piece of paper, they will revel in pouring large quantities of glue on the paper. Again, exploring these new materials is a sensory experience for them.

Characteristics of Children During the Organized Scribbler Phase

Because of increased cognitive, perceptual, and language development, children "begin to use their memory consciously and to learn memory strategies, such as repetition" (Bergen & Coscia, 2001, p. 30). During this period, children begin to say words. They can produce most vowel sounds and about half of the consonant sounds (Bergen & Coscia, 2001). Children have developed a vocabulary of about 50 to 400 words (Jalongo, 2004). Vocabulary is steadily increasing during this phase. They are able to understand more language that is verbally communicated to them than they are able to verbally communicate themselves (Allen & Marotz, 2007). Children are more visually focused on their work as they engage in various artmaking experiences. They can put objects together and take them apart, such as fitting large pegs into a peg board. Physically, they are able to stand and walk independently.

Art Experiences for the Organized Scribbler Phase

The art experiences described on the following pages can help develop the following skills necessary for literacy: hand-eye coordination, fine motor skills, visual perception and discrimination, and critical thinking. These art experiences meet various literacy benchmarks as well. These benchmarks were taken from the Mid-continent Research for Education and Learning website (2006). For more information on these benchmarks, see Appendix A.

Many art experiences can nurture literacy skills. The key is that they be engaging to the young child. The following suggestions incorporate materials that lend themselves to a sense of discovery and adventure for the young child. They are all open-ended experiences as well. It is imperative that an adult share in the learning experience with the child to expand the child's "zone of proximal development."

How Adults Can Facilitate Learning During the Organized Scribbler Phase

Adults should verbally point out to children shapes and lines to assist with language development and visual perception (for example, "this is a square," "this is a squiggly line"). Encourage children to tell you about their artwork. As you draw with the child, show him or her circles that are rounder, lines that are straighter, wider, thinner. Draw complex designs that will be coming soon in the child's development, such as circles surrounded by other circles. These serve as the building blocks to the more detailed drawings that will come in the next phase. They are also good preparation for formal writing that will begin to emerge as children get older.

Aesthetic Characteristics of Children in the Organized Scribbler Phase

Children tend to enjoy:

- Artwork with bright colors
- Looking at both abstract and realistic artwork
- Artwork that relates to real life
- Subject matter that is not frightening

These characteristics were found in Western children who viewed Western paintings. Cross-cultural research on aesthetic preferences of young children is sparse. But according to Newton & Kantner (1977), "Subject matter and color seem to be universally significant dimensions shaping aesthetic preferences, particularly among younger children" (p.172). Hart (1993) encourages us to acknowledge that different socio-cultural groups have different aesthetic values and responses. When viewing artworks, including both Western and non-Western, "adults play a vital role in determining what children notice about a particular work and how children feel about the very process of encountering works of art" (Dietrich & Hunnicut, 1948, p. 154). Visits to the art museum can be beneficial to the young toddler. Approaching the experiences in a multi-sensory way will make the experience more meaningful to the child (Shaffer and Danko-McGhee, 2004). Following the art experiences, we suggest multi-sensory games.

Art Appreciation and Criticism Games for Children in the Organized Scribbler Phase

These games focus on *play* and *conversations* (Cole & Schaefer, 1990). *Play* involves finding connections between an artwork and the viewer by using tangible objects. *Conversations* direct the child into talking about the artwork while focusing on details.

Children who engage in these games can become better consumers of art and can have higher-quality encounters with artworks. All of these games can be played in a museum setting or in a classroom with displays of a variety of art reproductions, both two dimensional and three dimensional. By engaging in such activities, children can begin to retell the stories seen in the pictures and start to construct their own stories through art. They can also describe the artwork through color, shape, and line, thereby developing visual perception and discrimination skills. Teachers can serve as role models by introducing new vocabulary. All of these games help develop literacy.

Art Experience 1: Water Designs

Language Art Benchmarks:

Reading Standard 5 (Level Pre-K)

- Understands that illustrations and pictures convey meaning

Listening and Speaking Standard 8 (Level Pre-K)

- Uses new vocabulary to describe feelings, thoughts, experiences, and observations
- Asks questions to obtain information
- Answers simple questions
- Listens for a variety of purposes (e.g., to gain and share information, to perform a task, for enjoyment, to learn what happened in a story, to converse with an adult or peer)
- Follows one- and two-step directions
- Listens to a variety of fiction, nonfiction, poetry, drama, rhymes, and songs

Suggested Vocabulary Words:

Mix, blend, color, red, blue, yellow, line

Related Children's Books:

See the Ocean by Estelle Condra

Related Artwork:

Look at Kandinsky's *Sea Battle* and talk about colors and lines in a language that the child understands. Other paintings of the sea and boats can be used as well. Have children compare their water designs with the various paintings.

Related Music:

Echoes of Nature: Ocean Waves—Natural Sounds of the Wilderness (Laserlight Series) Playing sounds of the ocean can help set the tone during this experience.

Materials Needed:

Overhead projector
Plexiglas to cover projector's glass surface
Glass tray filled with water
Strings and yarns
Lace
Food coloring
Cooking oil
Eye or medicine droppers
Netting
Pipe cleaners
Feathers
Any other transparent or semitransparent materials

Procedure:

1. Cover the overhead projector's glass surface with a piece of Plexiglas to protect it from water spills.
2. Place the glass tray filled with water on the Plexiglas-covered surface.
3. Turn on the projector to project light onto a screen or wall.
4. Invite the children to experiment with different materials by placing materials into the water tray and watching the projected image on the screen.
5. Encourage children to add drops of watercolor and oil to observe interesting results.
6. Add small pieces of strings and yarns and pipe cleaners twisted into interesting shapes.
7. Encourage children to add other materials for further explorations of transparent properties, semitransparent properties, opaqueness, and color mixing.
8. Guide the children into discussing what they see. Introduce new vocabulary words.

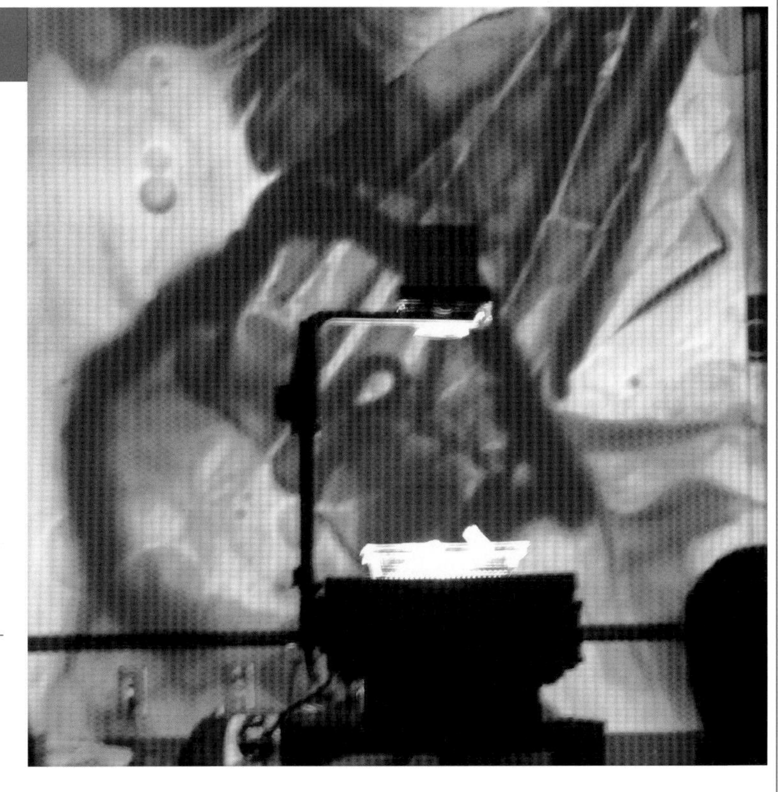

Table 2.1 Literacy Skills Nurtured in Water Designs

Visual Perception & Discrimination	Sequencing	Language Acquisition	Fine Motor	Gross Motor	Hand-Eye Coordination	Critical Thinking
●		●	●	●	●	●

What Children Will Learn:

- **Visual perception and discrimination**—Comparing and contrasting lines, colors, and shapes of different materials and patterns.
- **Language acquisition**—Using words to describe what they see after listening to the adult use descriptive words while facilitating this learning process.
- **Fine motor skills**—Manipulating different materials.
- **Hand-eye coordination**—Arranging objects in a water container.
- **Critical thinking**—Discussing their created image or comparing it to a selected artwork, such as the Kandinsky piece. Predicting whether the materials placed in the water will be transparent or opaque.

Art Experience 2: Painting on Plexiglas

Language Art Benchmarks:

Writing Standard 1

- Uses drawings to express thoughts, feelings, and ideas
- Uses writing tools and materials (e.g., pencils, crayons, chalk, markers, rubber stamps, computers, paper, cardboard, chalkboard)

Listening and Speaking Standard 8 (Level Pre-K)

- Uses new vocabulary to describe feelings, thoughts, experiences, and observations
- Uses descriptive language (e.g., color words; size words, such as bigger, smaller; shape words)
- Asks questions to obtain information
- Answers simple questions
- Listens for a variety of purposes (e.g., to gain and share information, to perform a task, for enjoyment, to learn what happened in a story, to converse with an adult or peer)
- Follows one- and two-step directions

Suggested Vocabulary Words:

Mix, blend, color, red, blue, yellow, orange, purple, green, line, brush, paint

Materials Needed:

Plexiglas sheets cut to a desirable size

Wooden stands to secure Plexiglas in an upright position

Assorted tempera paints, each mixed with liquid soap

Assorted paintbrushes

Water containers

Newspaper

Procedure:

1. Place a Plexiglas sheet in a wooden stand so that it is in an upright position.
2. Cover work area with newspaper.
3. Use paper plates as palettes and put a variety of tempera paints mixed with liquid soap on each. Soap will help the paint to adhere to the Plexiglas.
4. Proceed in a number of ways. For example, each child can paint individually on the Plexiglas or they can paint in pairs with each on opposite sides of the glass.
5. Place the Plexiglas in front of a window to show children the variety of colors and how light can affect them.
6. Point out various linear patterns and color combinations to the child to engage him or her in conversation.

Table 2.2 Literacy Skills Nurtured in Plexi Glass Painting

Visual Perception & Discrimination	Sequencing	Language Acquisition	Fine Motor	Gross Motor	Hand-Eye Coordination	Critical Thinking
●		●	●	●	●	●

What Children Will Learn:

- **Socialization**—Having a dialogue "in pictures," as each child responds to images painted by the child on the other side of the Plexiglas.
- **Color mixing and making various lines**—Using different colors and making lines using different brush sizes.
- **Exercising different muscle groups**—Using different muscle groups than they would working on a horizontal surface.
- **Fine motor skills**—Holding onto the paintbrush and drawing linear strokes across the Plexiglas.
- **Tracking and visual discrimination skills**—Following the lines of their markings; both skills (tracking and visual discrimination) are necessary for reading and writing.

Art Experience 3: Finger-Paint Monoprints I

Language Art Benchmarks:

Writing Standard 1

- Uses drawings to express thoughts, feelings, and ideas
- Uses writing tools and materials (e.g., pencils, crayons, chalk, markers, rubber stamps, computers, paper, cardboard, chalkboard)

Listening and Speaking Standard 8 (Level Pre-K)

- Uses new vocabulary to describe feelings, thoughts, experiences, and observations
- Uses descriptive language (e.g., color words; size words, such as bigger, smaller; shape words)
- Asks questions to obtain information
- Answers simple questions
- Listens for a variety of purposes (e.g., to gain and share information, to perform a task, for enjoyment, to learn what happened in a story, to converse with an adult or peer)
- Follows one- and two-step directions
- Listens to a variety of fiction, nonfiction, poetry, drama, rhymes, and songs

Suggested Vocabulary Words:

Mix, blend, color, red, blue, yellow, orange, purple, green, line, darker, lighter

Related Book to Read:

A Rainbow of My Own by Don Freeman

Related Music:

"Somewhere Over the Rainbow" from the *Wizard of Oz*

Materials Needed:

Large white sheets of paper
Assorted colors of finger paint
Apron or old shirt
Newspaper
Large cookie sheet or Styrofoam tray
Combs, tongue depressors, spatulas, Q-tips, etc.

Procedure:

1. Cover work area with newspaper.
2. Place a large Styrofoam tray on the work surface.
3. Drop a spoonful of a light color of finger paint (such as yellow) onto the Styrofoam tray.
4. Spread the finger paint over the surface of the tray.
5. Make linear patterns on this surface by using fingers, combs, spatulas, etc.
6. When the linear explorations are complete, clean hands for the next step.
7. Place a white sheet of paper over the finger-painted surface and gently rub the entire surface.
8. Pull the paper from the finger-painted surface and you have the first print.
9. Repeat process by putting the print aside to dry and using a darker color of finger paint. Make a new linear pattern and repeat steps 4 to 6.
10. After the new design is made with a new color, place the previously made print over the new finger-paint design and rub the entire surface.
11. Layers of color can be built up by repeating steps 3 to 8 and going from light to darker colors.
12. Leave the final print to dry when completed.

Table 2.3 Literacy Skills Nurtured in Mono Prints I and II

Visual Perception & Discrimination	Sequencing	Language Acquisition	Fine Motor	Gross Motor	Hand-Eye Coordination	Critical Thinking
●	●	●	●	●	●	●

What Children Will Learn:

- **Visual discrimination skills**—Learning to mix colors.
- **Hand-eye coordination and fine motor skills**—Using these skills (needed for writing) during the drawing process.
- **Sequencing skills and critical thinking**—Following the necessary steps to be successful with the printmaking process.
- **Vocabulary development**—Learning as adult uses descriptive language as new colors and linear patterns are made and as adult talks with the child about this creative process.

Art Experience 4: Finger-Paint Monoprints II

Language Art Benchmarks:

Writing Standard 1

- Uses drawings to express thoughts, feelings, and ideas
- Uses writing tools and materials (e.g., pencils, crayons, chalk, markers, rubber stamps, computers, paper, cardboard, chalkboard)

Listening and Speaking Standard 8 (Level Pre-K)

- Uses new vocabulary to describe feelings, thoughts, experiences, and observations
- Uses descriptive language (e.g., color words; size words, such as bigger, smaller; shape words)
- Asks questions to obtain information
- Answers simple questions
- Listens for a variety of purposes (e.g., to gain and share information, to perform a task, for enjoyment, to learn what happened in a story, to converse with an adult or peer)
- Follows one- and two-step directions
- Listens to a variety of fiction, nonfiction, poetry, drama, rhymes, and songs

Suggested Vocabulary Words:

Mix, blend, color, red, blue, yellow, orange, purple, green, line, darker, lighter

Materials Needed:

Large white sheets of paper

Assorted colors of finger paint

Apron or old shirt

Newspaper

Large cookie sheet or Styrofoam tray

Combs, tongue depressors, spatulas, Q-tips, etc.

Colored chalk

Procedure:

1. Cover work area with newspaper.
2. On white paper, draw a design of lines or scribbles using a variety of colored chalks. Put aside when finished.
3. Place a large Styrofoam tray on the work surface.
4. Drop a spoonful of a dark color of finger paint (such as black, blue, or purple) onto the Styrofoam tray.
5. Spread the finger paint over the surface of the tray.
6. Make linear patterns on this surface by using fingers, combs, spatulas, etc.
7. When the linear explorations are complete, clean hands for the next step.
8. Place your white sheet of paper with the chalk design face down over the finger-painted surface and gently rub the entire surface.
9. Pull the paper from the finger-painted surface. The chalk design will show through the finger-paint design to make rich layers of colors and patterns.
10. Discuss with the child the new colors and patterns made.
11. Leave the final print to dry when completed.

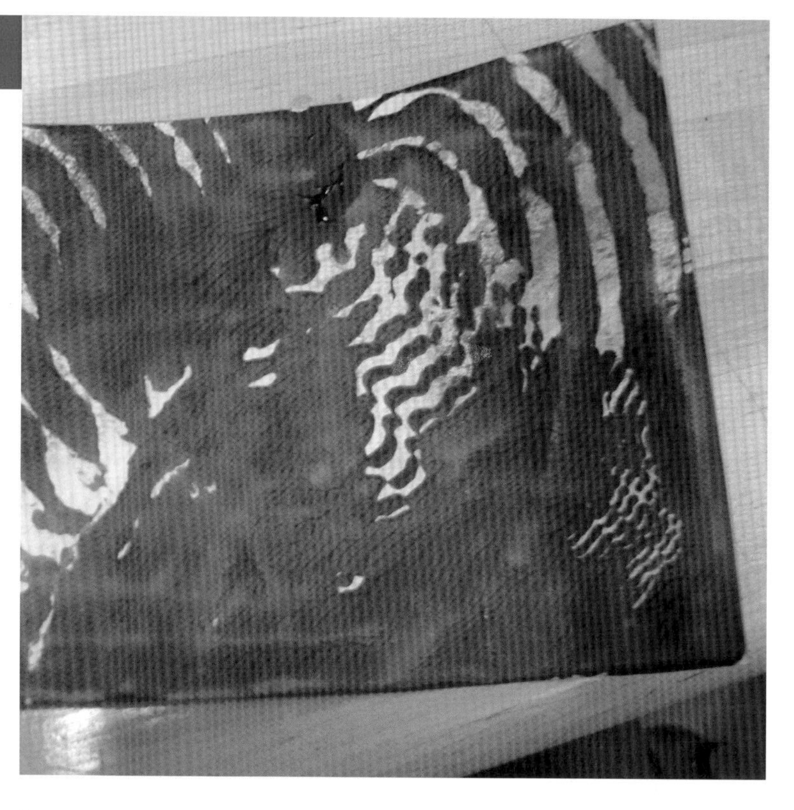

See Table 2.3

What Children Will Learn:

- **Visual discrimination skills**—Learning to mix colors.
- **Hand-eye coordination and fine motor skills**—Using these skills (needed for writing) during the drawing process.
- **Sequencing skills and critical thinking**—Following the necessary steps to be successful with the printmaking process.
- **Vocabulary development**—Learning as adult uses descriptive language as new colors and linear patterns are made and as adult talks with the child about this creative process.

Art Experience 5: Jell-O Paintings

Language Art Benchmarks:

Writing Standard 1

- Uses drawings to express thoughts, feelings, and ideas

Listening and Speaking Standard 8 (Level Pre-K)

- Uses new vocabulary to describe feelings, thoughts, experiences, and observations
- Uses descriptive language (e.g., color words; size words, such as bigger, smaller; shape words)
- Asks questions to obtain information
- Answers simple questions
- Listens for a variety of purposes (e.g., to gain and share information, to perform a task, for enjoyment, to learn what happened in a story, to converse with an adult or peer)
- Follows one- and two-step directions
- Listens to a variety of fiction, nonfiction, poetry, drama, rhymes, and songs

Suggested Vocabulary Words:

Color, red, blue, yellow, orange, purple, green, line, darker, lighter, sprinkle, smell

Related Books:

Old Black Fly by Jim Aylesworth. Have children pay attention to the visuals as the story is told to them.

Action Jackson by Jan Greenberg, Sandra Jordan, Robert A. Parker

Related Artwork:

Show any works by Jackson Pollock and discuss colors and lines using developmentally appropriate language.

Materials Needed:

Assorted boxes of Jell-O

White liquid glue

5-inch by 7-inch white poster board or blank index cards

Spoons

Newspaper

Procedure:

1. Read related books and show related artwork.
2. Cover work area with newspaper.
3. Do a scribble drawing using white liquid glue.
4. Before the glue dries, sprinkle on a variety of Jell-O powders using a spoon.
5. Watch the powder become more vibrant as the Jell-O touches the glue. Talk to the child about the color and how it becomes brighter when it touches the glue. Talk about the fragrance of each color.
6. Shake off any excess Jell-O powder.
7. Place Jell-O painting in a place to dry.

What Children Will Learn:

- **Multi-sensory experience**—Guessing what color the powdered Jell-O will turn when it comes in contact with the wet glue. Exploring the raised surface when the project is dry.
- **Hand-eye coordination and fine motor skills**—Sprinkling the powdered Jell-O onto the wet glue.
- **Visual discrimination skills**—Using different powder colors and watching the mixing of Jell-O and glue.
- **Language**—Describing the fragrance of the Jell-O and the resulting linear patterns that are made.

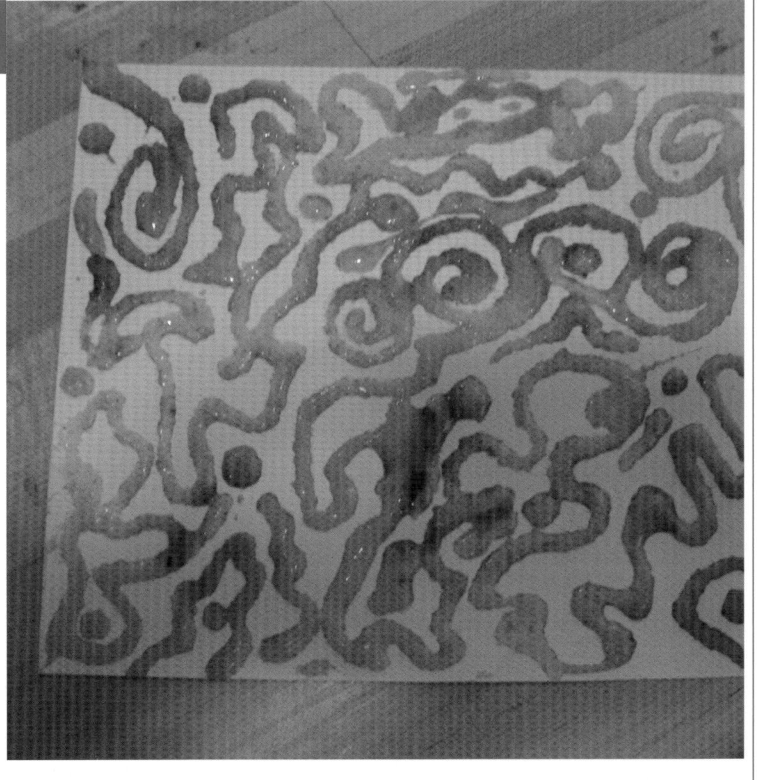

Table 2.4 Literacy Skills Nurtured in Jello Painting

Visual Perception & Discrimination	Sequencing	Language Acquisition	Fine Motor	Gross Motor	Hand-Eye Coordination	Critical Thinking
●		●	●		●	●

Art Experience 6: Dream Clouds

Language Art Benchmarks:

Listening and Speaking Standard 8 (Level Pre-K)

- Uses new vocabulary to describe feelings, thoughts, experiences, and observations
- Uses descriptive language (e.g., color words; size words, such as bigger, smaller; shape words)
- Asks questions to obtain information
- Answers simple questions
- Listens for a variety of purposes (e.g., to gain and share information, to perform a task, for enjoyment, to learn what happened in a story, to converse with an adult or peer)
- Follows one- and two-step directions
- Listens to a variety of fiction, nonfiction, poetry, drama, rhymes, and songs

Suggested Vocabulary Words:

Mix, blend, color, red, blue, yellow, orange, purple, green, darker, lighter, soft, squishy, cloud

Related Books:

Little Cloud by Eric Carle

It Looks Like Spilt Milk by Charles G. Shaw

I Call It Sky by Will C. Howell

Cloud Dance by Thomas Locker

Clouds by Henry Fountain

Related Music:

Music Inspired by the Beauty of the Sky, a CD by Kevin Kendle

Materials Needed:

Plastic zip-lock sandwich bag

Food coloring or liquid water colors

Shaving cream

Procedure:

1. Before doing this activity, lie down in the grass with the children and talk about clouds, their shapes, colors, sizes. Read stories (listed below) about clouds and listen to music (listed below) inspired by clouds.
2. Open up one sandwich bag and fill halfway with shaving cream.
3. Have each child choose two colors of food coloring, then squeeze a few drops of each color into the shaving cream.
4. Seal the bag, making sure all of the air is released.
5. Have the child squeeze the closed bag to mix the colors.
6. Discuss how it feels with the children while introducing vocabulary words, such as squishy, soft.
7. Observe your "cloud" when the mixing is done.
8. If you have reproductions of outdoor paintings, have the children try to find their cloud in each of the paintings, e.g., rainy day clouds, sunny day clouds.

Related Artwork:

Have children view any painting with clouds. A simple game can be played by matching photographs of clouds to clouds found in each painting. Chart weather conditions and cloud formations for a week to study how clouds relate to various weather conditions.

Table 2.5 Literacy Skills Nurtured in Dream Cloud Experience

Visual Perception & Discrimination	Sequencing	Language Acquisition	Fine Motor	Gross Motor	Hand-Eye Coordination	Critical Thinking
●		●	●		●	●

What Children Will Learn:

- **Proportions and color mixing**—Placing various colors into the zip-lock bag.
- **Visual discrimination and critical thinking skills**—Comparing their cloud in the bag to clouds found in various art reproductions.
- **Fine motor and hand-eye coordination skills**—Placing the foam in the bag and then sealing it.

Art Experience 7: Fragrant Clay

Language Art Benchmarks:

Listening and Speaking Standard 8 (Level Pre-K)

- Uses new vocabulary to describe feelings, thoughts, experiences, and observations
- Uses descriptive language (e.g., color words; size words, such as bigger, smaller; shape words)
- Asks questions to obtain information
- Answers simple questions
- Listens for a variety of purposes (e.g., to gain and share information, to perform a task, for enjoyment, to learn what happened in a story, to converse with an adult or peer)
- Follows one- and two-step directions
- Listens to a variety of fiction, nonfiction, poetry, drama, rhymes, and songs

Suggested Vocabulary Words:

Mix, blend, color, red, blue, yellow, orange, purple, green, sprinkle

Materials Needed:

Mixing bowl
Mixing spoon
Measuring cup
Self-rising flour
Salt
Kool-Aid
Warm water
Objects made out of clay

Procedure:

1. Read the book *Little Lump of Clay* by D. Engel. Look at objects made from clay and talk about them with the child.
2. Measure 1 cup of flour and 1 cup of salt and place into mixing bowl.
3. Add 1 packet of Kool-Aid.
4. Stir in warm water gradually.
5. Mix until it resembles Play-Doh. Mixture should not stick to the fingers.
6. Encourage child to create any form desired using this clay mixture.
7. Talk with the child about what the clay feels like. Introduce vocabulary words, such as soft, squishy.
8. Try assorted flavors of Kool-Aid for a variety of colors.

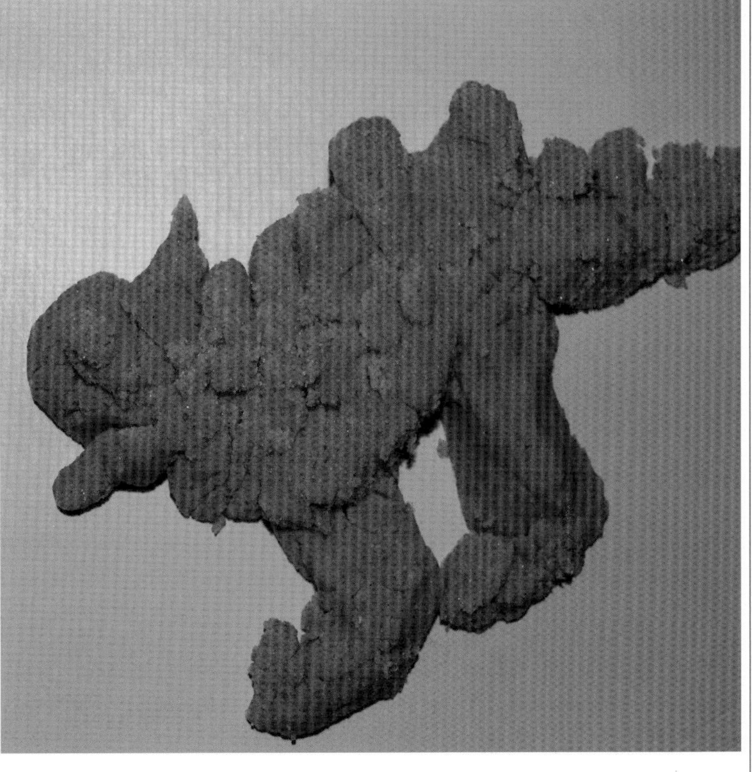

Table 2.6 Literacy Skills Nurtured in Fragrant Clay Experience

Visual Perception & Discrimination	Sequencing	Language Acquisition	Fine Motor	Gross Motor	Hand-Eye Coordination	Critical Thinking
	●		●	●	●	

What Children Will Learn:

- **Sequencing skills**—Follow the required steps to make the clay.
- **Fine and gross motor skills, and hand-eye coordination**—Mixing the ingredients.

Game 1: Color Match

Standards:

Listening and Speaking Standard 8 (Level Pre-K)

- Uses descriptive language (e.g., color words; size words, such as bigger, smaller; shape words)
- Follows one- and two-step directions

Suggested Vocabulary Words:

Color, red, blue, yellow, orange, purple, green, line, darker, lighter, match

Materials Needed:

Paint-color samples from the hardware store

Art reproductions displayed in the room at children's eye level

Procedure:

1. Display various painting reproductions in the classroom. They should be at child level.
2. Give each child a 1-inch square of color. Paint samples from the hardware store are perfect for this activity because of the wide spectrum of colors.
3. Ask the child to find the color in the selected artworks.
4. As each color is discovered, instruct the child to place the color sample on the floor in front of the artwork. Confirm choices made.
5. As a studio extension, have children paint a picture using these color choices.

What Children Will Learn:

- **Visual discrimination skills**—Scanning an artwork to find the color they are looking for. Learning about the subtleties and nuances of colors.
- **Language skills**—Describing the location of the color in the artwork.
- **Critical thinking**—Examining the subtleties and nuances of color to find the right match.

Table 2.7 Literacy Skills Nurtured in Color Match Experience

Visual Perception & Discrimination	Sequencing	Language Acquisition	Fine Motor	Gross Motor	Hand-Eye Coordination	Critical Thinking
●		●				●

Game 2: Match the Object to the Painting

Standards:

Listening and Speaking Standard 8 (Level Pre-K)

- Uses new vocabulary to describe feelings, thoughts, experiences, and observations
- Uses descriptive language (e.g., color words; size words, such as bigger, smaller; shape words)
- Follows one- and two-step directions

Suggested Vocabulary Words:

Match, feather, lace, pearls (depending on the objects chosen for this game)

Materials Needed:

Basket containing a variety of materials, such as feather, pearl necklace, fabric swatches

Art reproductions displayed in the classroom at children's eye level

Procedure:

1. Give children baskets containing the items that can be found in a selected group of art reproductions, such as lace, ribbons of various colors, fabric swatches of different textures and colors.
2. Ask children to match the articles in their baskets to articles shown in the artworks. After matches are made, instruct children to share with others where the items can be found in the corresponding artworks.

What Children Will Learn:

- **Visual discrimination, language, and critical thinking**—Looking carefully at an artwork to match their object to items in the artwork.

Table 2.8 Literacy Skills Nurtured in Match the Object to the Painting

Visual Perception & Discrimination	Sequencing	Language Acquisition	Fine Motor	Gross Motor	Hand-Eye Coordination	Critical Thinking
●		●				●

The Story Scribbler

Making a connection between scribbling and words can be a powerful literacy acquisition experience for children learning new words. A child talking about scribbles creates an important teachable moment for adults to engage in conversations with the child. By doing this, the adult observer gains insight into the child's thoughts and can appropriately engage him or her in expanding and enriching his or her thoughts.

When children use a variety of art media in a more meaningful way, as they are beginning to do in this phase, they should be encouraged to tell stories to further nurture literacy because children's pictures represent their true interests and the ideas they wish to explore. In this phase the child's interest is used as the focal point in the literacy experience.

Children continue to explore lines and shapes during this phase and their work begins to take on the appearance of abstract (nonrealistic) designs. They begin to combine circles, crosses, lines, and other shapes and symbols from their earlier scribbling to produce new and more complex images. "Some of the marks represent not objects but movements, sounds and feelings—a visual representation of dramatic play" (Anning, 1997, p. 228).

Children begin to assign names to their scribbles and to tell stories as they draw. This naming involves a change from kinesthetic (pure pleasure of movement and exploration of material) to symbolic thinking, where drawings become representations of something the child has experienced. For instance, a circle can represent a self-portrait or a set of squiggly lines can represent the ocean. The lines that children create start to become borders around spaces that can be recognized as shapes. As these shapes emerge, they are named and renamed.

Children increasingly acquire understanding that images can communicate socially shared meanings. . . . Opportunity to share drawings with peers and adults, and the praise received when marks on paper can be explained as depictions of people and objects, further encourage children to interweave visual, verbal, and gestural cues. (Anning, 1997, p. 31)

When children are working with three-dimensional materials, these same tendencies to recognize and name shapes are evident. When working with clay, "forming bridges from coils and making short columns stand up are early examples of children's growing realization that they can actually build with clay. They may practice these skills over and over again by making a series of 'bridges' and 'rockets'" (Kolbe, 1997, p. 8). The configurations that children make in clay will remind them of something and they will begin to name their work. Various sound effects and talking accompany the explorations in this medium.

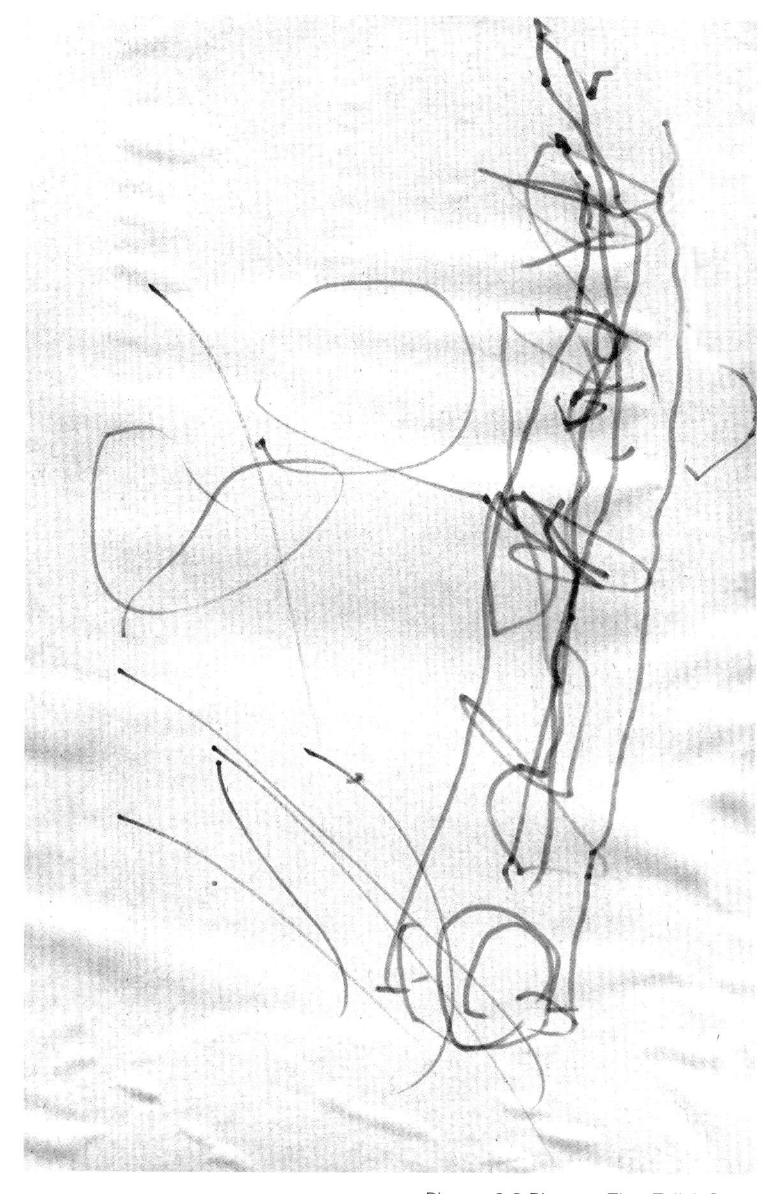

Picture 2.8 Pictures That Tell A Story

Additional Characteristics of the Story Scribbler

1. Spends more time mark making
2. Frequently changes the name of the scribble in the drawing process
3. Has increased concentration
4. Has more intentional placement of marks
5. Has better fine motor control and uses the whole hand to draw
6. Is able to speak in sentences and has developed a 1,000-word vocabulary; is able to engage in conversation (Jalongo, 2004)
7. Can point to a requested shape, such as circle or square (Allen & Marotz, 2007)
8. Can sort objects according to color, shape, or size (Allen & Marotz, 2007)
9. Can recite nursery rhymes (Allen & Marotz, 2007)
10. Physically, children have much better developed fine motor skills and hand-eye coordination

Art Experiences for the Story Scribbler Phase

Children should be encouraged to draw, but there are various other ways to engage them in art experiences. Providing a variety of materials for visual, tactile, kinesthetic, and olfactory experiences is the first step in developing aesthetic awareness (Stokrocki, 1984). Therefore, experiences should not be limited only to drawing, but also should include working with materials that will give the child a three-dimensional experience. Once again, these activities are open-ended to allow children to experience them in their own ways.

How Adults Can Facilitate Growth During the Story Scribbler Phase

Adults can draw or construct in parallel with the child, creating designs like those of the child, but with more sophistication (Wilson & Wilson, 1981). They can engage in conversations about the artwork, being specific in their comments to help introduce children to new vocabulary. This dialogue, by helping the child examine his or her artistic creations, contributes to the development of not only the child's artistic process but also underlying thinking skills.

Aesthetic Characteristics of Children in the Story Scribbler Phase

Western children enjoy viewing and creating abstract and realistic artworks that contain bright colors. Western children also begin to prefer certain artworks because of real-life associations. They do not like subject matter that frightens them.

Aesthetic experiences involve:

> ***complex aspects of human behavior including perceptions, attention to and discrimination of sensory information, values, emotions, interpretations of meaning, and the intricate relationships of all these factors to each other. (Newton & Kantner, 1997, p. 168)***

Decoding visual imagery is a learned ability that is conditioned by the socio-cultural context. For example, young children in Africa have spatial interpretation challenges (Mundy-Castle, 1960; Hudson, 1960). However, Chinese children have no problem decoding three dimensionality that is portrayed in paintings (Kindler, 1997). Therefore:

> ***the familiarity of the culture with objects and ideas in the images also influences perception; and . . . the degree of strictness of the culture affects individual openness and ability to recognize depth cues. (Newton & Kantner, 1997, p. 169)***

Because of socio-cultural conditioning, all children may not react the same when viewing a work of art. However, children in this phase are more mature and have a more extensive vocabulary, enabling them to engage in more challenging art criticism experiences. Nevertheless, try not to overwhelm the child. Play the games after the story scribbler art experiences while viewing only one or two artworks to keep the experience manageable.

Art Experience 8: Transparent Color Weavings

Language Art Benchmarks:

Listening and Speaking Standard 8 (Level Pre-K)

- Speaks clearly enough to be understood by unfamiliar adults and uses appropriate levels of volume, tone, and inflection
- Uses new vocabulary to describe feelings, thoughts, experiences, and observations
- Uses descriptive language (e.g., color words; size words, such as bigger, smaller; shape words)
- Asks questions to obtain information
- Answers simple questions
- Follows conversation rules (e.g., taking turns, making relevant comments, staying on topic) when talking with peers and adults
- Listens for a variety of purposes (e.g., to gain and share information, to perform a task, for enjoyment, to learn what happened in a story, to converse with an adult or peer)
- Understands messages in conversations (e.g., responds differently based on purpose of messages in conversation; attends and responds to conversations)
- Follows one- and two-step directions

Suggested Vocabulary Words:

Cellophane, weave, over, under, color, scrunch

Materials Needed:

Landscape/construction fencing mesh
Colored cellophane
Colored tissue paper
Yarns
Ribbons
Lace
Any other transparent colored linear materials suitable for weaving through fence mesh
Clear packing tape.

Procedure:

1. Cut landscape mesh to fit over a window and secure with clear packing tape.
2. Cut tissue and/or cellophane into long strips or scrunch into long ropes and weave through landscape mesh.
3. Weave through the mesh any other colored transparent materials.
4. Use two different colors of cellophane to weave through the mesh to observe the mixing of colors.
5. Use opaque weaving materials so that children can observe the different properties of all the materials.
6. Talk with the children about the materials used and the weaving process. Introduce new descriptive words during this conversation.

Table 2.9 Literacy Skills Nurtured in Color Weaving Experience

Visual Perception & Discrimination	Sequencing	Language Acquisition	Fine Motor	Gross Motor	Hand-Eye Coordination	Critical Thinking
●		●	●		●	●

What Children Will Learn:

- **Weaving**—Using different materials for weaving. Succeeding at weaving because of the large openings in the construction fencing. Taking a good first step to more complicated weavings later.
- **Visual discrimination, fine motor, and hand-eye coordination skills**—Selecting materials to place into the mesh.
- **Critical thinking**—Making decisions about color choices and placement.
- **Language skills**—Learning new words as the adult talks about the weaving process.

Art Experience 9: Light Table: Color Mixing Experiences

Language Art Benchmarks:

Listening and Speaking Standard 8 (Level Pre-K)

- Speaks clearly enough to be understood by unfamiliar adults and uses appropriate levels of volume, tone, and inflection
- Uses new vocabulary to describe feelings, thoughts, experiences, and observations
- Uses descriptive language (e.g., color words; size words, such as bigger, smaller; shape words)
- Asks questions to obtain information
- Answers simple questions
- Follows conversation rules (e.g., taking turns, making relevant comments, staying on topic) when talking with peers and adults
- Listens for a variety of purposes (e.g., to gain and share information, to perform a task, for enjoyment, to learn what happened in a story, to converse with an adult or peer)
- Understands messages in conversations (e.g., responds differently based on purpose of messages in conversation; attends and responds to conversations)
- Follows one- and two-step directions

Suggested Vocabulary Words:

Light, color, pattern, magnifying glass, feel, touch

Materials Needed:

Light table that is child's height

Assorted colors of acetate sheets

Scissors

Assorted colors of transparent items such as glass stones (2-inch diameter), plastic shapes, plastic beads

Feathers

Any other transparent or semitransparent item

Procedure:

1. Turn on light table. To prevent tripping, make sure cord is not exposed.
2. Place assorted colored transparent items on the table.
3. Ask children to explore these materials by overlapping different objects to observe color mixing. Suggest they organize the colored glass stones into various patterns to practice sequencing skills.
4. Facilitate discussion about new colors and patterns made by the child.

Table 2.10 Literacy Skills Nurtured in the Light Table Experience

Visual Perception & Discrimination	Sequencing	Language Acquisition	Fine Motor	Gross Motor	Hand-Eye Coordination	Critical Thinking
●	●	●	●			●

What Children Will Learn:

- **Exploring objects from different ways**—Viewing materials from a different vantage point. Exploring objects in different ways because the light source comes from beneath the objects.
- **Develop sequencing skills**—Sorting various materials, thereby developing sequencing skills that are important in reading and writing.
- **Visual discrimination and fine motor skills**—Exploring new color combinations and selecting items according to colors.
- **Critical thinking**—Sorting, especially if sequencing the colored stones into various color patterns.
- **Language skills**—Learning new vocabulary words from the adult who facilitates this process.

Art Experience 10: Computer Art

Language Art Benchmarks:

Writing Standard 1 (Level Pre-K)

- Knows that writing, including pictures, letters, and words, communicates meaning and information
- Uses drawings to express thoughts, feelings, and ideas

Listening and Speaking Standard 8 (Level Pre-K)

- Speaks clearly enough to be understood by unfamiliar adults and uses appropriate levels of volume, tone, and inflection
- Uses new vocabulary to describe feelings, thoughts, experiences, and observations
- Uses descriptive language (e.g., color words; size words, such as bigger, smaller; shape words)
- Asks questions to obtain information
- Answers simple questions
- Follows conversation rules (e.g., taking turns, making relevant comments; staying on topic) when talking with peers and adults
- Listens for a variety of purposes (e.g., to gain and share information, to perform a task, for enjoyment, to learn what happened in a story, to converse with an adult or peer)
- Understands messages in conversations (e.g., responds differently based on purpose of messages in conversation; attends and responds to conversations)
- Follows one- and two-step directions

Suggested Vocabulary Words:

Computer, mouse, screen, draw

Computer Art Programs

Children in the story scribbler phase are ready to explore artistic programs on the computer. The following software programs include a large drawing surface with a user-friendly menu of tools and special effects.

Kid Pix Studio—This program uses sound effects and music along with capabilities of movement (the images children create can move on the screen). Children can also make a movie using their own graphics.

HyperStudio—Children can create their own images with sound effects and animation.

Crayola: Make a Masterpiece—Has the same features as both Kid Pix Studio and HyperStudio.

Disney's Magic Artist—Has the same features as both Kid Pix Studio and HyperStudio.

Be aware that many technology programs and websites incorporate activities that invite children to color within a template. These activities don't allow children the freedom to fully exercise their visual perceptions, fine motor skills, and cognitive processes (such as critical thinking and problem solving). Avoid these programs to ensure that the child is engaging in a quality learning experience.

Table 2.11 Literacy Skills Nurtured in the Computer Art Experience

Visual Perception & Discrimination	Sequencing	Language Acquisition	Fine Motor	Gross Motor	Hand-Eye Coordination	Critical Thinking
●			●		●	●

What Children Will Learn:

- **Visual discrimination, hand-eye coordination, and fine motor skills**—Moving the mouse to make marks on the computer monitor.
- **Critical thinking skills**—Using programs that offer open-ended creative art experiences.

Art Experience 11: Painting With Different Tools

Language Art Benchmarks:

Writing Standard 1 (Level Pre-K)

- Uses drawings to express thoughts, feelings, and ideas
- Uses writing tools and materials (e.g., pencils, crayons, chalk, markers, rubber stamps, computers, paper, cardboard, chalkboard)
- Uses forms of emergent writing (e.g., scribble writing, random symbols, random letter-like marks) to represent ideas

Listening and Speaking Standard 8 (Level Pre-K)

- Speaks clearly enough to be understood by unfamiliar adults and uses appropriate levels of volume, tone, and inflection
- Uses new vocabulary to describe feelings, thoughts, experiences, and observations
- Uses descriptive language (e.g., color words; size words, such as bigger, smaller; shape words)
- Asks questions to obtain information
- Answers simple questions
- Follows conversation rules (e.g., taking turns, making relevant comments; staying on topic) when talking with peers and adults
- Listens for a variety of purposes (e.g., to gain and share information, to perform a task, for enjoyment, to learn what happened in a story, to converse with an adult or peer)
- Understands messages in conversations (e.g., responds differently based on purpose of messages in conversation; attends and responds to conversations)
- Follows one- and two-step directions

Materials Needed:

Blue, red, yellow, black, and white tempera paint

Rolls of white paper (approximately 48 inches by 50 inches)

Paper plates

Assorted painting tools such as feather duster, sponge-tip brush, sponge roller, small mop heads

Newspaper

Procedure:

1. Cover work area with newspaper.
2. Place paints onto paper plates (one color per plate).
3. Roll white paper over newspaper.
4. Paint using the assorted painting tools and also experiment with mixing colors.
5. Work on tables, on the floor, or outside on a sidewalk. Children need ample space to conduct their explorations.
6. Facilitate this process by talking with the children about new colors they've made and discussing the various textured markings that the tools make.

Suggested Vocabulary Words:

Texture, line, sponge, rough, bumpy

Table 2.12 Literacy Skills Nurtured in Painting with Different Tools

Visual Perception & Discrimination	Sequencing	Language Acquisition	Fine Motor	Gross Motor	Hand-Eye Coordination	Critical Thinking
●		●	●		●	

What Children Will Learn:

- **Visual discrimination, fine motor, and hand-eye coordination skills**—Using the various painting tools and exploring the variety of markings that they make.
- **Language skills**—Learning new vocabulary words as adult describes the markings and new colors made on the painted surface.

Art Experience 12: Drawing With Sticks

Language Art Benchmarks:

Writing Standard 1 (Level Pre-K)

- Uses drawings to express thoughts, feelings, and ideas
- Uses writing tools and materials (e.g., pencils, crayons, chalk, markers, rubber stamps, computers, paper, cardboard, chalkboard)

Listening and Speaking Standard 8 (Level Pre-K)

- Speaks clearly enough to be understood by unfamiliar adults and uses appropriate levels of volume, tone, and inflection
- Uses new vocabulary to describe feelings, thoughts, experiences, and observations
- Uses descriptive language (e.g., color words; size words, such as bigger, smaller; shape words)
- Asks questions to obtain information
- Answers simple questions
- Follows conversation rules (e.g., taking turns, making relevant comments; staying on topic) when talking with peers and adults
- Listens for a variety of purposes (e.g., to gain and share information, to perform a task, for enjoyment, to learn what happened in a story, to converse with an adult or peer)
- Understands messages in conversations (e.g., responds differently based on purpose of messages in conversation; attends and responds to conversations)
- Follows one- and two-step directions

Suggested Vocabulary Words:

Stick, line, draw, squiggly, zigzag, curvy, straight

Materials Needed:

1/2–inch-wide dowel sticks cut to approximately the height of a small child's shoulder

Assorted colors of markers

Duct tape

White paper in a roll (approximately 48 inches by 50 inches)

Procedure:

1. Read the story *The Squiggle* by C.L. Schaefer (1999). Talk about different lines in the story. Have children make their own lines using a stick.
2. Use duct tape to attach one marker to the end of a dowel stick. Make sure that the tip of the marker extends beyond the tip of the dowel stick.
3. Repeat the previous procedure using different marker colors. If desired attach two, three, or four markers to the stick.
4. Roll out paper on the floor or sidewalk.
5. Ask children to take a dowel stick and begin to draw and experiment with line patterns while standing.
6. Facilitate conversation about the various lines that are drawn, using descriptive vocabulary such as swirly, zigzag, curvy, straight.

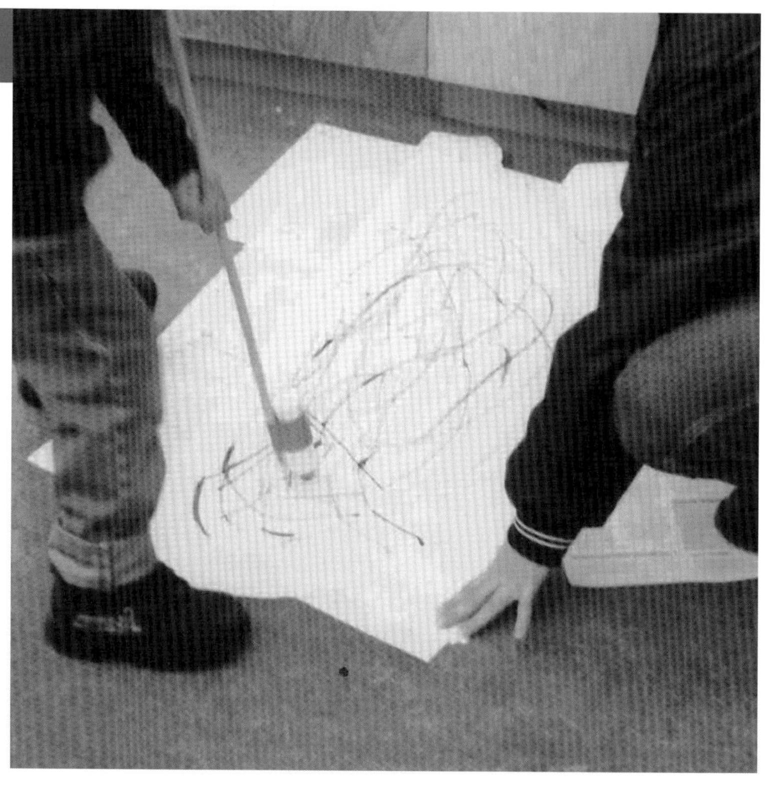

Table 2.13 Literacy Skills Nurtured in Drawing with Sticks

Visual Perception & Discrimination	Sequencing	Language Acquisition	Fine Motor	Gross Motor	Hand-Eye Coordination	Critical Thinking
●		●	●	●	●	

What Children Will Learn:

- **Different drawing tool and markings**—Experimenting with a different drawing tool that can produce a variety of lines. Learning that marks do not have to be made in a traditional way.
- **Fine motor skills**—Drawing linear patterns.
- **Gross motor skills**—Drawing with the whole arm.
- **Hand-eye coordination**—Negotiating movements and making markings on the paper.
- **Visual discrimination**—Creating and examining a drawing.
- **Language skills**—Conversing with an adult about the work.

Art Experience 13: Rainbows in a Bag

Language Art Benchmarks:

Listening and Speaking Standard 8 (Level Pre-K)

- Uses new vocabulary to describe feelings, thoughts, experiences, and observations
- Uses descriptive language (e.g., color words; size words, such as bigger, smaller; shape words)
- Answers simple questions
- Follows one- and two-step directions
- Understands basic conversational vocabulary

Suggested Vocabulary Words:

Soft, squishy, color, mix, blend, rainbow

Materials Needed:

Hair gel
Wooden spoon
3 small bowls
Red, yellow, and blue food coloring or liquid water colors
Heavy zipper-closure plastic bag
Masking tape
Overhead projector (optional)

Procedure:

1. Read *A Rainbow of My Own* by Don Freeman.
2. Look at Morris Louis's painting *Point of Tranquility*.
3. Play the song "Somewhere Over the Rainbow" while children are working.
4. Put hair gel into bowls and thoroughly mix in food coloring or liquid water colors. Each bowl will have a separate color.
5. Have children spoon two or more gel colors into a plastic bag.
6. Zip the bag closed, making sure air is out. Secure with masking tape.
7. Squeeze and knead the bag of colors and watch as the colors blend.
8. Place bags on an overhead projector's glass surface to view "rainbows" on the screen. Children can manipulate the colors while watching the screen.
9. Facilitate conversation about new color explorations.

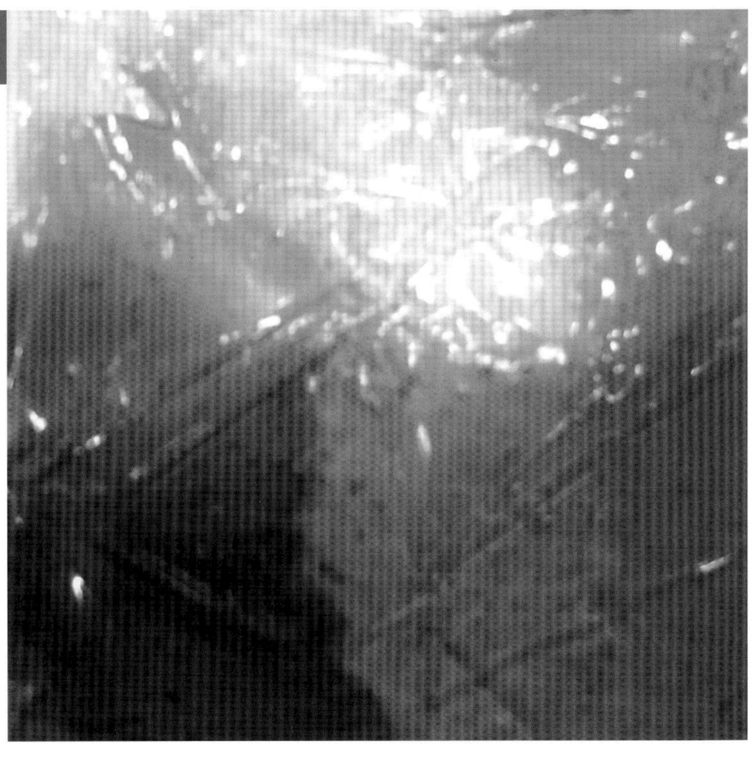

Table 2.14 Literacy Skills Nurtured in the Rainbows in a Bag Experience

Visual Perception & Discrimination	Sequencing	Language Acquisition	Fine Motor	Gross Motor	Hand-Eye Coordination	Critical Thinking
●		●	●		●	●

What Children Will Learn:

- **Cause and effect and making predictions**—Mixing colors. This activity serves as a precursor to more formal critical thinking skills by providing cause and effect experiences that prepare children to make predictions. Making predictions is an important skill that is often associated with reading and understanding inferences within text.
- **Visual discrimination, fine motor, and hand-eye coordination skills**—Mixing gels, combining colors, and sealing the bag.
- **Language acquisition and new vocabulary**—Talking with the adult as they engage in this activity. Talking about textures and mixing colors. Listening as the adult models the use of new vocabulary words to describe the texture of the plastic bag filled with gel and new colors made during the process.

Art Experience 14: Action Paintings

Language Art Benchmarks:

Listening and Speaking Standard 8 (Level Pre-K)

- Uses new vocabulary to describe feelings, thoughts, experiences, and observations
- Answers simple questions
- Follows one- and two-step directions
- Understands basic conversational vocabulary
- Uses descriptive language (e.g., color words; size words, such as bigger, smaller; shape words)
- Listens to a variety of fiction, nonfiction, poetry, drama, rhymes, and songs

Suggested Vocabulary Words:

Wiggle, swing, sway, dribble, splash, drop, splatter

Materials Needed:

White butcher paper

Tempera paints (red, blue, yellow, white, black)

Sturdy plastic bags

Scissors

Reproductions of Jackson Pollock paintings

Books: *Old Black Fly* by Jim Ayelsworth, *Action Jackson* by Jan Greenberg, Sandra Jordan, and Robert A. Parker

Good action music of your choice

Newspaper

String or cord

Procedure:

1. Read the story *Old Black Fly* by Jim Ayelsworth.
2. Talk about the images in the book and compare them to the work of Jackson Pollock. Also, read the book *Action Jackson* by Greenberg , Jordan, and Parker.
3. Have children guess how the paintings were made. Talk about what the paintings look like to them. Have them count the many different colors they see.
4. Roll out white butcher paper over newspaper on the floor or on an outside sidewalk.
5. Fill plastic bags with tempera paint, one color per bag.
6. Tie closed with strong string or cord.
7. Give each child a bag filled with the paint. Instruct child to hold the bag over the paper on the floor.
8. With scissors, cut a small incision into the bottom of the bag.
9. Have children swing bags over the paper as the paint dribbles in a Jackson Pollock fashion.
10. Play music to inspire children while they engage in this activity.
11. When complete, have a discussion with the children about the new colors they've made by mixing colors.
12. Have them give a title to their collaborative painting.

Table 2.15 Literacy Skills Nurtured in Action Painting

Visual Perception & Discrimination	Sequencing	Language Acquisition	Fine Motor	Gross Motor	Hand-Eye Coordination	Critical Thinking
●			●	●	●	●

What Children Will Learn:

- **Fine and gross motor skills, and hand-eye coordination**—Moving paint bags across the surface of the paper.
- **Visual discrimination skills**—Looking for new colors they've made.
- **Critical thinking skills**—Coming up with a title for their painting.
- **Social skills**—Working collaboratively with others to complete the painting project.

Art Experience 15: Painting With Baby Oil and Q-tips

Language Art Benchmarks:

Writing Standard 1(Level pre-K)

- Uses drawings to express thoughts, feelings, and ideas
- Uses writing tools and materials (e.g., pencils, crayons, chalk, markers, rubber stamps, computers, paper, cardboard, chalkboard)

Listening and Speaking Standard 8 (Level Pre-K)

- Uses new vocabulary to describe feelings, thoughts, experiences, and observations
- Answers simple questions
- Follows one- and two-step directions
- Understands basic conversational vocabulary
- Uses descriptive language (e.g., color words; size words, such as bigger, smaller; shape words)

Suggested Vocabulary Words:

Q-tip, draw, transparent, line, straight, curved, squiggly, zigzag, circular

Materials Needed:

Q-tips
Baby oil
Small cups
Newspaper
Construction paper in a variety of colors

Procedure:

1. Cover work area with newspaper.
2. Place colored construction paper on newspaper.
3. Fill a small cup with baby oil.
4. Using a Q-tip dipped in the baby oil, draw on the construction paper.
5. When complete, hang the drawing in the window. Areas that are drawn with the oil will be transparent.
6. Talk with the child about the drawing. Discuss why the oil makes the paper transparent. Introduce new vocabulary words that are age appropriate.

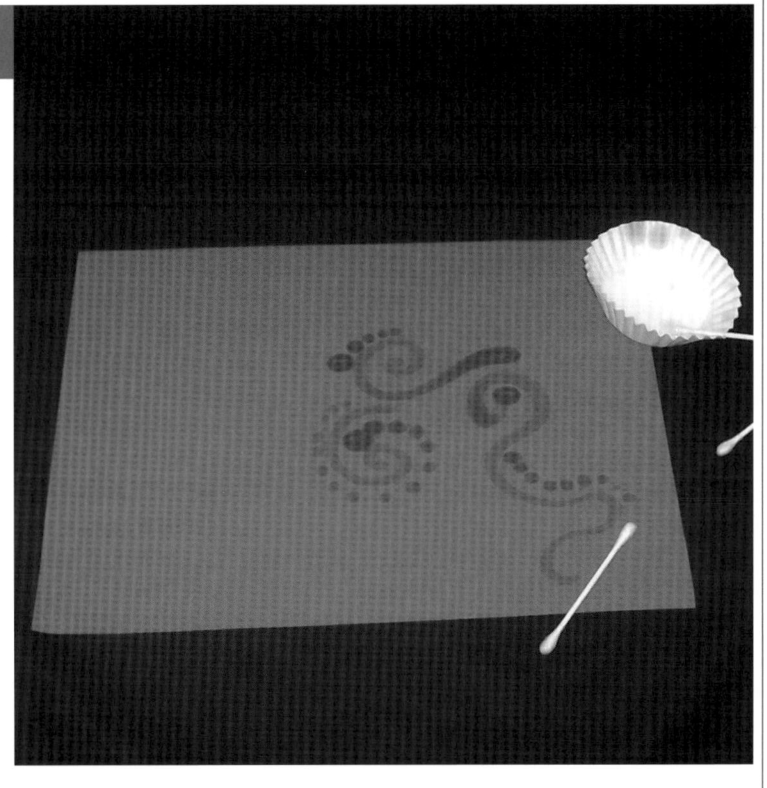

Table 2.16 Literacy Skills Nurtured in Painting with Baby Oil

Visual Perception & Discrimination	Sequencing	Language Acquisition	Fine Motor	Gross Motor	Hand-Eye Coordination	Critical Thinking
●		●	●		●	

What Children Will Learn:

- **A new medium for drawing.**
- **Fine motor, hand-eye coordination, and visual discrimination**—Refining these skills as they draw.
- **The properties of materials and their cause and effect.**
- **New vocabulary words**—Exploring and talking about the process of drawing with oil.

Art Experience 16: Painting With Fingertip Brushes

Language Art Benchmarks:

Writing Standard 1(Level Pre-K)

- Uses drawings to express thoughts, feelings, and ideas
- Uses writing tools and materials (e.g., pencils, crayons, chalk, markers, rubber stamps, computers, paper, cardboard, chalkboard)

Listening and Speaking Standard 8 (Level Pre-K)

- Uses new vocabulary to describe feelings, thoughts, experiences, and observations
- Answers simple questions
- Follows one- and two-step directions
- Understands basic conversational vocabulary
- Uses descriptive language (e.g., color words; size words, such as bigger, smaller; shape words)

Suggested Vocabulary Words:

Fingertip, brush, paint, line, color, straight, curved, circular

Materials Needed:

Fingertip brushes (can be purchased at school supply stores or websites—see Appendix C)

Assorted liquid watercolors

Newspaper

Watercolor paper

Small containers or cups

Procedure:

1. Cover work area with newspaper.
2. Fill small containers with liquid watercolors. Use one color per container.
3. Place watercolor paper onto newspaper.
4. Put fingertip brushes onto fingers.
5. Dip the tip of each brush into a color and paint.
6. Explore color mixing with the children. Talk about the creation of new colors. Use descriptive words to describe the process of painting. Encourage children to describe the process as well.

What Children Will Learn:

- **Color mixing and creating new colors.**
- **Fine motor skills, the pincer grip, hand-eye coordination, and visual discrimination**—Nurturing these skills, all of which are important for handwriting.

Table 2.15 Literacy Skills Nurtured in Painting with Fingertip Brushes

Visual Perception & Discrimination	Sequencing	Language Acquisition	Fine Motor	Gross Motor	Hand-Eye Coordination	Critical Thinking
●			●		●	

Art Experience 17: Sand Tray on Light Table

Language Art Benchmarks:

Writing Standard 1 (Level pre-K)

- Uses drawings to express thoughts, feelings, and ideas
- Uses writing tools and materials (e.g., pencils, crayons, chalk, markers, rubber stamps, computers, paper, cardboard, chalkboard)

Listening and Speaking Standard 8 (Level Pre-K)

- Uses new vocabulary to describe feelings, thoughts, experiences, and observations
- Uses descriptive language (e.g., color words; size words, such as bigger, smaller; shape words)
- Answers simple questions
- Follows one- and two-step directions
- Understands basic conversational vocabulary

Suggested Vocabulary Words:

Sand, coarse, gritty, tool, light

Materials Needed:

Large, flat glass or plastic container (approximately 20 inches by 24 inches)

Sand (try to use sand that has a low dust level, such as Jurassic Sand)

Light table

Paint scrapers (can be purchased from Discount School Supplies—see Appendix C)

Photographs of Zen rock gardens, such as Ryoanji in Kyoto, Japan

Photographs of Andy Goldsworthy's work with sand

Procedure:

1. Fill a glass or plastic tray with sand about 1-inch deep.
2. Spread sand evenly in tray.
3. Place tray on light table.
4. Hang photographs of Zen rock gardens and Goldsworthy's art above the light table. Talk about these art forms with the child.
5. Using a paint scraper, draw into the sand. As sand is scraped away in linear patterns, it will reveal the light from below.
6. Have children experiment by using different scrapers that will produce different line patterns.
7. Have children compare their linear patterns to the designs in the Zen gardens. How are they the same? How are they different? Have children describe the lines that they are making using descriptive words such as swirl, wiggly, curved, etc.

Table 2.18 Literacy Skills Nurtured in the Sand Tray Experience

Visual Perception & Discrimination	Sequencing	Language Acquisition	Fine Motor	Gross Motor	Hand-Eye Coordination	Critical Thinking
●		●	●		●	●

What Children Will Learn:

- **The properties of sand.**
- **Using a variety of tools for drawing.**
- **Hand-eye coordination, visual perception, fine motor, and pincer grip skills**—Scraping sand enhances all of these skills, which assist with handwriting.
- **Vocabulary development**—Talking about the different lines they produce.
- **Critical thinking**—Contrasting and comparing their linear patterns with those found in Zen gardens and Goldsworthy's pieces.

Art Experience 18: Colored Plastic Bottles on Light Table

Language Art Benchmarks:

Listening and Speaking Standard 8 (Level Pre-K)

- Uses new vocabulary to describe feelings, thoughts, experiences, and observations
- Uses descriptive language (e.g., color words; size words, such as bigger, smaller; shape words)
- Answers simple questions
- Follows one- and two-step directions
- Understands basic conversational vocabulary

Suggested Vocabulary Words:

Plastic, shape, overlap, blend, transparent, light

Materials Needed:

Different colors of plastic bottles or containers cut into a variety of shapes

Light table

Procedure:

1. Turn on light table.
2. Place the cut-up plastic bottle shapes and forms onto the table.
3. Have children explore these forms and colors by arranging them in different ways. Overlapping pieces can create new colors and forms.
4. Introduce new vocabulary words, such as overlap and underneath.

What Children Will Learn:

- **Mixing colors using different materials.**
- **Vocabulary development**—Learning new vocabulary words while creating new colors and shapes with the materials.
- **Fine motor, visual discrimination, and hand-eye coordination skills**—Making arrangements with the materials.

Table 2.19 Literacy Skills Nurtured in the Plastic Bottles Experience

Visual Perception & Discrimination	Sequencing	Language Acquisition	Fine Motor	Gross Motor	Hand-Eye Coordination	Critical Thinking
●		●	●		●	

Game 1: Match the Emotion

Language Art Benchmarks:

Writing Standard 1 (Level Pre-K)

- Knows that writing, including pictures, letters, and words, communicates meaning and information

Listening and Speaking Standard 8 (Level Pre-K)

- Speaks clearly enough to be understood by unfamiliar adults and uses appropriate levels of volume, tone, and inflection
- Uses new vocabulary to describe feelings, thoughts, experiences, and observations
- Uses descriptive language (e.g., color words; size words, such as bigger, smaller; shape words)
- Asks questions to obtain information
- Answers simple questions
- Follows conversation rules (e.g., taking turns, making relevant comments; staying on topic) when talking with peers and adults
- Listens for a variety of purposes (e.g., to gain and share information, to perform a task, for enjoyment, to learn what happened in a story, to converse with an adult or peer)
- Understands messages in conversations (e.g., responds differently based on purpose of messages in conversation; attends and responds to conversations)
- Follows one- and two-step directions

Materials Needed:

Reproductions of portrait paintings that display various facial expressions

Photographs of various facial expressions mounted on cardboard

Procedure:

This game helps children identify their feelings. Give each child color photographs of faces with different expressions. For younger children, it is better to give one face at a time to alleviate frustration. Ask children to find a painting or sculpture in the room with the same facial expression as the picture(s) they have in their hands. As each match is found, ask the children to place their color photo on the floor in front of the corresponding artwork. After matches are made, encourage children to talk about why they made their choices. Read *Today I Feel Silly* by Jamie Lee Curtis for a wonderful extension to this activity, as it further explores emotions with young children.

Suggested Vocabulary Words:

Emotion, happy, sad, angry, jealous, feelings

What Children Will Learn:

- **Different emotions and the various ways they can be expressed.**
- **Language development**—Describing the emotions conveyed in an artwork.
- **Critical thinking and visual perception skills**—Searching for matches to the emotions portrayed on cards.

Table 2.20 Literacy Skills Nurtured in the Match the Emotion Game

Visual Perception & Discrimination	Sequencing	Language Acquisition	Fine Motor	Gross Motor	Hand-Eye Coordination	Critical Thinking
●		●				●

Game 2: Painting Puzzles

Language Art Benchmarks:

Listening and Speaking Standard 8 (Level Pre-K)

- Speaks clearly enough to be understood by unfamiliar adults and uses appropriate levels of volume, tone, and inflection
- Uses new vocabulary to describe feelings, thoughts, experiences, and observations
- Uses descriptive language (e.g., color words; size words, such as bigger, smaller; shape words)
- Asks questions to obtain information
- Answers simple questions
- Follows conversation rules (e.g., taking turns, making relevant comments; staying on topic) when talking with peers and adults
- Listens for a variety of purposes (e.g., to gain and share information, to perform a task, for enjoyment, to learn what happened in a story, to converse with an adult or peer)
- Understands messages in conversations (e.g., responds differently based on purpose of messages in conversation; attends and responds to conversations)
- Follows one- and two-step directions

Suggested Vocabulary Words:

Puzzle, shape, color, line, fit

Materials Needed:

Postcards of artworks cut up into large puzzle pieces

Procedure:

Cut postcard reproductions of artworks into puzzle pieces. Give each child one piece of the puzzle and then lead him or her into the gallery that contains the painting that is the match for the puzzle. If in a classroom setting, art reproductions can be on display.

Ask the child to find the painting in the room that looks like the piece of the puzzle in their hand. Once found, have the child place the puzzle piece on the floor in front of the painting.

After children match their puzzle piece to the painting, ask them to join their puzzle pieces with the other children's puzzle pieces to create one puzzle that corresponds to the artwork they were asked to match. This is a self-correcting game as children will check their puzzle to see if it matches the corresponding artwork.

What Children Will Learn:

- **Working cooperatively with peers**— Facing the challenge of putting the puzzle together.
- **Fine motor and hand-eye coordination skills**—Piecing the puzzle together.
- **Visual discrimination skills**—Matching up the puzzles pieces to fit.

Table 2.21 Literacy Skills Nurtured in Painting Puzzles

Visual Perception & Discrimination	Sequencing	Language Acquisition	Fine Motor	Gross Motor	Hand-Eye Coordination	Critical Thinking
●			●		●	

Game 3: Sound Effects to a Painting

Language Art Benchmarks:

Listening and Speaking Standard 8 (Level Pre-K)

- Speaks clearly enough to be understood by unfamiliar adults and uses appropriate levels of volume, tone, and inflection
- Understands messages in conversations (e.g. responds differently based on purpose of messages in conversation; attends and responds to conversations)
- Follows one- and two-step directions

Suggested Vocabulary Words:

Sound, animals (introduce different animal names that apply to the artwork)

Materials Needed:

An artwork that shows an environment for animals

A variety of stuffed animals

Procedure:

Use an artwork that shows an environment for animals. Paintings of animals can be used, but it is best to choose paintings that do not show animals so children can imagine which kinds of animals might live in the environment depicted. Distribute to the children stuffed animals that might be representative of animals that would live in the environment portrayed in the painting. Have children think about the sound their animal makes. Tell children that, at the count of three, they should make the sound of their animal, thus providing sound effects to the artwork.

What Children Will Learn:

- **Critical thinking skills—** Attempting to make the sounds of the animal they are given.

Table 2.22 Literacy Skills Nurtured in Sound Effects to a Painting Game

Visual Perception & Discrimination	Sequencing	Language Acquisition	Fine Motor	Gross Motor	Hand-Eye Coordination	Critical Thinking
						●

Summary

Early mark-making experiences in the form of scribbles identify the beginning of graphic development for young children. Through scribbling, children:

- Develop socially, emotionally, cognitively, and physically
- Develop self-concept, self-esteem, and self-discipline
- Communicate ideas and construct knowledge
- Enjoy and appreciate their own creative expressions
- Develop independent work habits
- Develop language and concept building

When children are involved in the creative process, they have many opportunities to develop language, problem-solving skills, memory, and visual perception. These art experiences show us the profound connections between children's development and the creative arts, as we see again and again how the visual arts stimulate the child's growth in every area: physical, emotional, social, and intellectual.

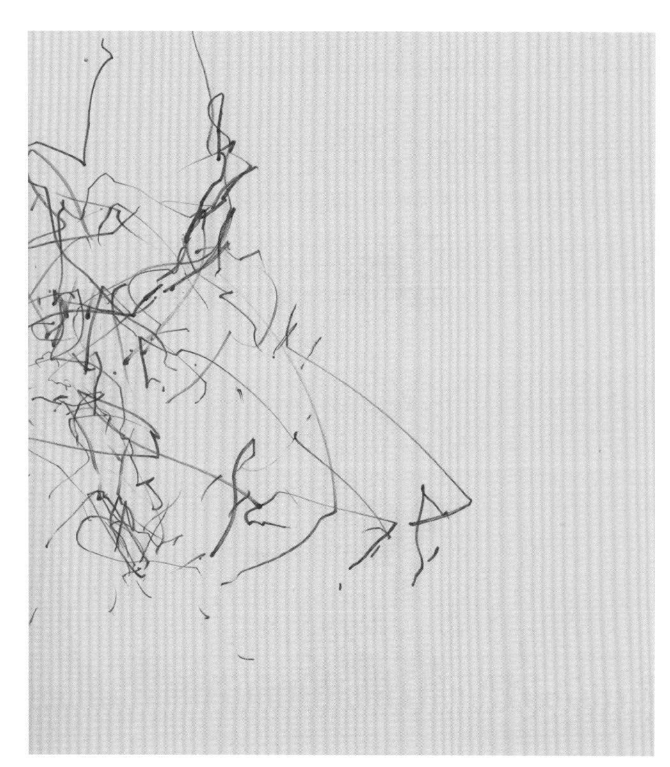

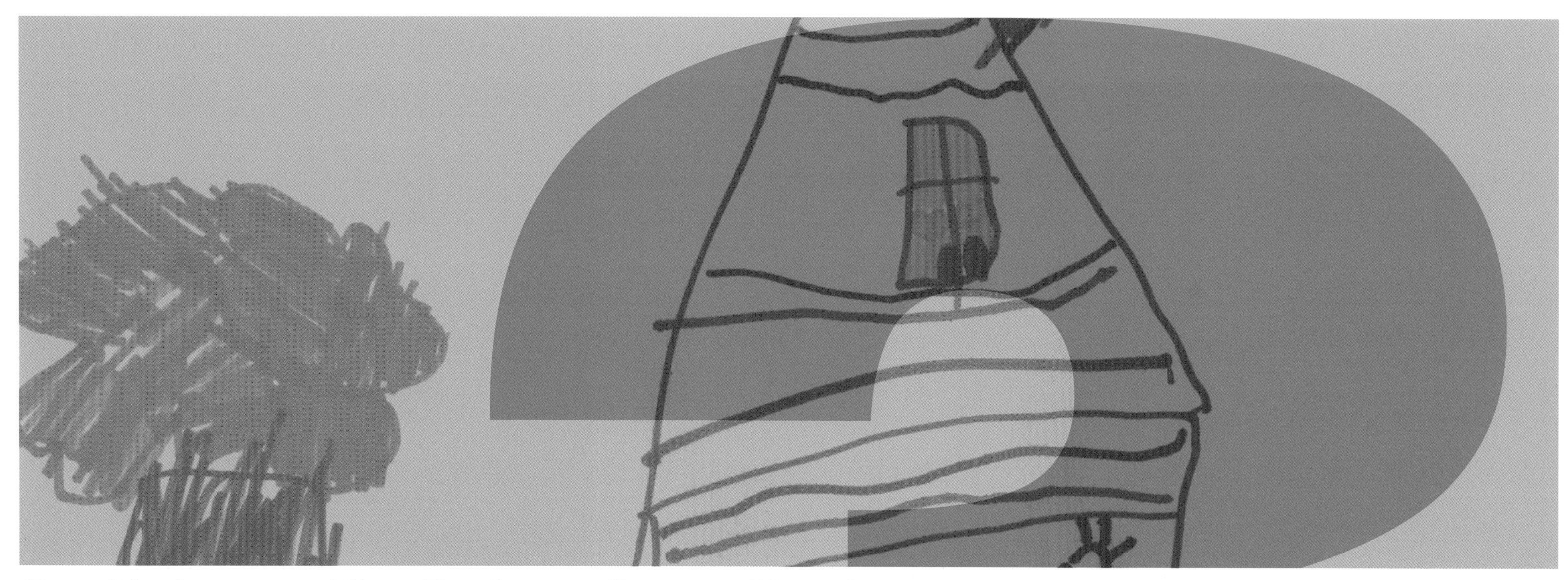

Graphic Imagery That Begins to Convey Meaning

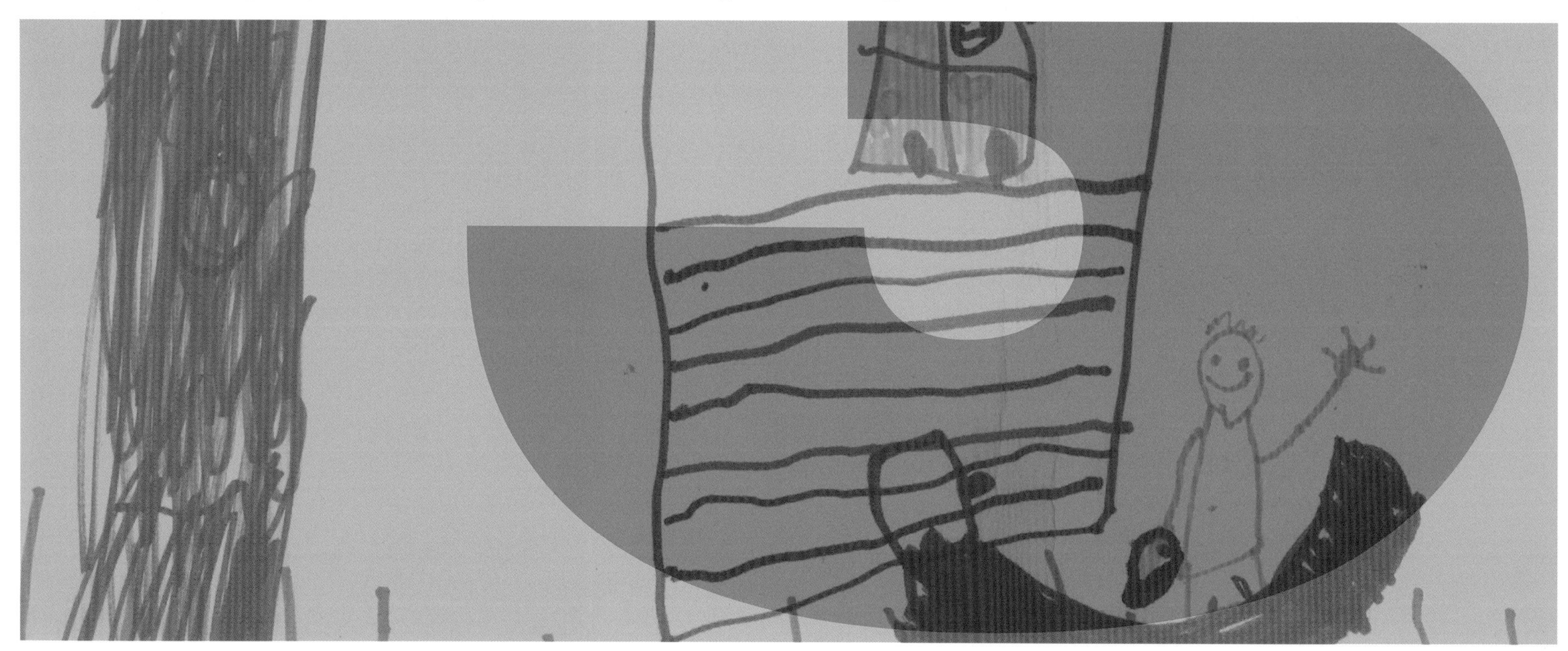

Characteristics of Children Who Draw to Convey Meaning

Picture 3.1: Circles for Hands and Feet

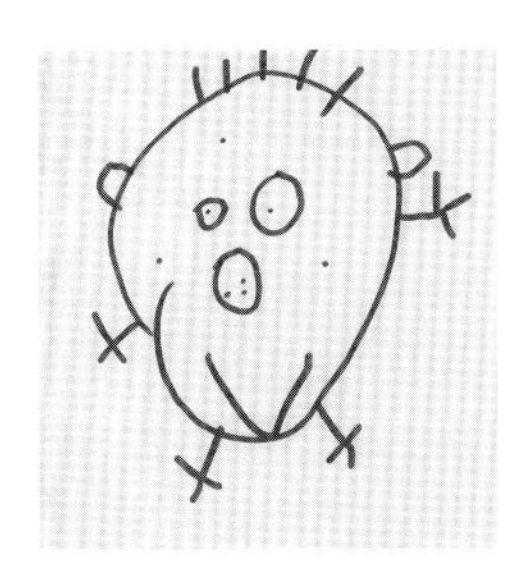

Picture 3.2: Tadpole

"In their early attempts to represent people, places, and objects, children draw what they know, a codified version of what they see" (Anning, 1997, p. 229).

During this phase (graphic imagery that conveys meaning) children's drawings serve as vehicles for conveying meaning and "can be shared socially and appear to be independent of verbal narrative or supporting gestural cues" (Kindler, 1997, p. 31). Because of their practice using various drawing tools to make a variety of marks, children's drawings have become more complex. Children are eager to offer a verbal or gestural account of their work when they feel it is necessary (Kindler & Darras, 1994; Kindler, 1997; Kindler & Thompson, 1994; and Thompson & Bales, 1991). The human form begins to emerge and typically includes one unit that symbolizes a head and torso with arms and legs attached (See pictures 3.1 and 3.2). Sometimes children have difficulty attaching these limbs, but they resolve these problems as they perfect their drawing skills.

Typically, arms stick straight out from the head/body unit. Body parts are often exaggerated and are out of proportion with the rest of the body. For example, the head may be the biggest part of the figure with very small appendages attached. The figure typically looks top heavy. Because children in this stage are still developing their graphic vocabulary, one symbol may represent many things or ideas. For example, a hand or foot is drawn as a circle with spokes surrounding it. As children progress, they will differentiate symbols and extend their graphic vocabulary. By the time a child is 3, he or she is typically able to draw a circle. This form begins in the story scribbler phase. Squares are typically not drawn until around age 5 and triangles appear around age 6. It is inappropriate to push children to draw these shapes before they are developmentally ready. These shapes will emerge as children explore the various symbols and linear patterns that evolve out of their scribbles and art experiences. Children also learn a great deal from their peers. Scribbles take on new meanings and become symbols that represent something.

In their early attempts to represent people, places, and objects, children draw what they know, a codified version of what they see.

(Anning, 1997)

Symbols drawn during this phase are usually out of proportion and appear to be unanchored. In other words, symbols are placed haphazardly on the drawing surface. Children often draw in a "stream of consciousness" way—they put down whatever comes to mind. While drawing, the child often rotates the paper and draws objects that do not relate to each other. Also, by rotating the paper, the child draws symbols that are sideways and upside down.

When children want to express more with their writing … the act of drawing itself provides a useful scaffold to story writing.

(Baghban, 2007)

Children during this stage tend to use colors of their choice, resulting in unique color applications. For example, trees can be pink and water can be purple. Images tend to be exciting as the child uses his or her creative license to execute the artwork. In a free-spirited way, children enjoy mixing colors to make new ones and to marvel at their creations.

Cognitively, children are becoming more sophisticated as they continue to create new symbols to signify various objects they have observed in their environment. Language skills become more advanced and they are able to have more extensive conversations about their artistic creations. Children are now able to produce more elaborate sentence structures (Allen & Marotz, 2007). Adults should model descriptive language to help children develop vocabulary and language, and to acquire ways to describe their own work.

At this phase children learn that what is known or experienced can be symbolically represented by mark making (creating drawings). They can draw how they think or feel about an object, which sometimes leads to exaggeration, but also helps foster creativity andfantasy exploration.

The Literacy Connection

During this phase, children's letter and number symbols exhibit the same type of development that their drawings do. Children typically do not start writing in a coherent and clear manner, but rather interject individual letters and numbers into their artwork to represent a concept, thought, or a big idea (Clay, 1987; Dyson, 1993). As children continue to explore these letters and numbers, they try to replicate adult-like writing behavior. This is evident when children incorporate traditional literacy symbols, like letters or numbers, into their artwork. The more language and literacy children acquire in their daily interactions, the more they show evidence of language use in their artwork. Perhaps children's drawings serve as a rehearsal for text writing (Temple, Nathan & Burris, 1982; Zulasky, 1982). We see a pattern of change as children subtly replace images with the written word. This does not mean that children discontinue their drawing experiences. Instead they begin to write more as they draw.

When children want to express more with their writing … the act of drawing itself provides a useful scaffold to story writing. Drawing helps children organize their ideas for expression in story writing. (Baghban, 2007, p. 22)

Children traverse between these communication systems, writing and drawing, a process that Harste, Burke, and Woodward (1984) identify as *negotiation.* They suggest that this negotiation process can help us understand how children use symbols to communicate in various ways. "Border skirmishes between art and writing, which arise as a result of negotiation, may in fact be a key to both our and the child's understanding and growth in literacy" (Harste, Burke & Woodward, 1984, p. 65).

Suggested Art Experiences

In this section, along with Language Art Benchmarks, we also include the National Visual Art Standards for the activities (see Appendix B for more detail). They are introduced in this chapter because they begin with kindergarten-age children—the approximate age of children in this phase.

Not all of the following experiences focus on drawing because it is important for young children to use three-dimensional materials as a "language." Just as much can be communicated with three-dimensional materials as with drawing. In fact, these experiences, "allow them to convey concepts about the three dimensional world which are impossible or difficult for them to depict through drawing and painting" (Kolbe, 1997, p. 3). Children who have had ample experience using three-dimensional materials "have been encouraged 'to see,' are able to use clay (or other materials) in increasingly complex ways" (Kolbe, 1997, p. 8).

These experiences are meant to foster learning and serve as launch pads for literacy acquisition. It is key that the adult becomes a co-explorer with the child during these experiences to help the child build from his or her knowledge base.

Aesthetic Abilities

Children's aesthetic abilities remain basically the same in this phase as in the previous one. However, their critical thinking skills are more sophisticated and these children are therefore capable of engaging in more challenging aesthetic games.

Art Appreciation and Criticism Games for Children in this Phase

The four games described at the end of this chapter require cognitive sophistication and are therefore suitable for older children, ages 5 to 6. As artworks are selected for these games, the teacher should bear in mind that children in this age group tend to prefer both abstract and realistic art works with bold colors. Good-quality picture books (Caldecott winners are a great starting point) and reproductions of artworks are also suitable to use with these children.

Art Experience 1: Musical Paints

Language Art Benchmarks:

Writing Standard 1(Level Pre-K)

- Knows that writing, including pictures, letters, and words, communicates meaning and information
- Uses drawings to express thoughts, feelings, and ideas
- Uses forms of emergent writing (e.g., scribble writing, random symbols, random letter-like marks) to represent ideas
- Uses writing tools and materials (e.g., pencils, crayons, chalk, markers, rubber stamps, computers, paper, cardboard, chalkboard)

Reading Standard 5 (Level Pre-K)

- Understands that illustrations and pictures convey meaning

Listening and Speaking Standard 8 (Level Pre-K)

- Uses new vocabulary to describe feelings, thoughts, experiences, and observations
- Uses descriptive language (e.g., color words; size words, such as bigger, smaller; shape words)
- Follows one- and two-step directions

National Visual Arts Standards:

Understanding and Applying Media, Techniques, and Processes

- Knows the difference between materials and techniques
- Describes how different materials, techniques, and processes cause different responses
- Uses different media, techniques, and processes to communicate ideas, experiences, and stories
- Uses art materials and tools in a safe and responsible manner

Materials Needed:

Assorted paint colors

Newspaper

Assorted painting and drawing tools (Q-tips, brushes, sticks, charcoal, oil pastels, chalk, colored pencils, etc.)

Small water containers

Musical selections of your choice (have a variety available)

Procedure:

1. Cover a long table with newspaper.
2. Put a sheet of paper at each child's place.
3. Place a different drawing or painting tool at each place.
4. Tell children not to paint or draw until they hear the music begin. They paint or draw with the tool provided in front of them as long as the music continues. They must stop when the music stops.
5. When the music stops, tell children to return the tool to the proper place on the table. Have them pick up their paper with both hands, and listen for directions: "Move one seat to the right. Do not begin painting or drawing until the music begins."
6. When the music begins, tell them to paint or draw for as long as they hear the music, then stop painting or drawing when the music stops.
7. Repeat steps 5 through 7.

Suggested Vocabulary Words:

Feelings, color names (such as red, yellow, blue)

Table 3.1 Literacy Skills Nurtured in Musical Paints Experience

Visual Perception & Discrimination	Sequencing	Language Acquisition	Fine Motor	Gross Motor	Hand-Eye Coordination	Critical Thinking
●		●	●		●	●

What Children Will Learn:

- **Listening skills**—Discerning how different music can convey different moods and emotions.
- **Visual perception and discrimination**—Using different tools and creating of differing line patterns.
- **Language acquisition**—Hearing words in the songs.
- **Fine motor skills**—Using different tools (skills needed for writing).
- **Hand-eye coordination**—Using tools that require coordinating hand movements on paper.
- **Critical thinking**—Translating the mood of the music and transferring it in graphic form onto their paper.

Art Experience 2: Painting With Dirt

Language Art Benchmarks:

Writing Standard 1(Level pre-K)

- Knows that writing, including pictures, letters, and words, communicates meaning and information
- Uses drawings to express thoughts, feelings, and ideas
- Uses forms of emergent writing (e.g., scribble writing, random symbols, random letter-like marks) to represent ideas
- Uses writing tools and materials (e.g., pencils, crayons, chalk, markers, rubber stamps, computers, paper, cardboard, chalkboard)

Reading Standard 5 (Level Pre-K)

- Understands that illustrations and pictures convey meaning

Listening and Speaking Standard 8 (Level Pre-K)

- Uses new vocabulary to describe feelings, thoughts, experiences, and observations.
- Uses descriptive language (e.g., color words; size words, such as bigger, smaller; shape words)
- Follows one- and two-step directions

National Visual Arts Standards:

Understanding and Applying Media, Techniques, and Processes

- Knows the difference between materials and techniques
- Describes how different materials, techniques, and processes cause different responses
- Uses different media, techniques, and processes to communicate ideas, experiences, and stories
- Uses art materials and tools in a safe and responsible manner

Suggested Vocabulary Words:

Texture, gritty, rough, ochre, rust

Materials Needed:

Assorted colors of ground-up dirt (have children gather dirt at home and discuss the different colors of dirt they bring in)

Small cups

Water

White liquid glue

Brushes

Newspaper

White or black construction paper

The book *Mud* by Wendy Cheyette Lewison

Examples of Australian Aboriginal Papunya or bark paintings

Examples of prehistoric cave paintings

Procedure:

1. Read the story *Mud* by Wendy Cheyette Lewison.
2. Talk about how people can paint with mud.
3. Look at various artworks that were painted with mud, such as Australian Aboriginal Papunya paintings and prehistoric cave drawings.
4. Have children look at all of the colors of dirt that they brought. Discuss making dirt into paint.
5. Place each color of finely ground dirt into a separate container.
6. Add water and a tablespoon of white glue and stir until the mixture is the consistency of ketchup.
7. Cover a work table with newspaper. Place cups of dirt paint, water cups, and brushes on the table.
8. Ask children to experiment with painting using the different colors of dirt paint and any size of white or black construction paper. Talk about the differences in dirt colors.

Table 3.2 Literacy Skills Nurtured in Painting with Dirt

Visual Perception & Discrimination	Sequencing	Language Acquisition	Fine Motor	Gross Motor	Hand-Eye Coordination	Critical Thinking
●		●	●		●	

What Children Will Learn:

- **Cause and effect**—Mixing paint.
- **Visual discrimination**—Noticing that dirt comes in different colors. Using the paintbrush or stick to create images. Comparing and contrasting the lines drawn and the dirt colors.
- **Language acquisition**—Discussing their artwork.
- **Fine motor skills**—Using paintbrushes and sticks, which facilitates writing.
- **Hand-eye coordination**—Using tools that require coordinating movements on paper.

Art Experience 3: Plunger Prints

Language Art Benchmarks:

Writing Standard 1 (Level Pre-K)

- Knows that writing, including pictures, letters, and words, communicates meaning and information
- Uses writing tools and materials (e.g., pencils, crayons, chalk, markers, rubber stamps, computers, paper, cardboard, chalkboard)

Listening and Speaking Standard 8 (Level Pre-K)

- Uses new vocabulary to describe feelings, thoughts, experiences, and observations.
- Uses descriptive language (e.g., color words; size words, such as bigger, smaller; shape words)
- Follows one- and two-step directions

National Visual Arts Standards:

Understanding and Applying Media, Techniques, and Processes

- Knows the difference between materials and techniques
- Describes how different materials, techniques, and processes cause different responses
- Uses different media, techniques, and processes to communicate ideas, experiences, and stories
- Uses art materials and tools in a safe and responsible manner

Suggested Vocabulary Words:

Plunger, circle, overlap, pattern, repeat, print.

Materials Needed:

Sink plungers (these have shorter handles than standard plungers) with different sizes of rubber cups

Assorted colors of tempera paints

Pie tins

Roll of white paper (or color of your choice)

Procedure:

1. Read *Round, Round, Round* by Tana Hoban.
2. Have the children look for and identify round objects in the room.
3. Roll out white paper to cover a work table.
4. Pour assorted tempera paints into pie tins, one color per tin.
5. Place one sink plunger into each color of paint.
6. Press sink plunger onto the white paper to leave a print.
7. Repeat process using different plunger sizes and paint colors.
8. Cover the entire white paper. Talk about the different sizes and colors of circles with the children.

What Children Will Learn:

- **Learning about shapes**—Noticing shapes and integrating them into their artwork.
- **Visual discrimination skills**—Noting the different colors and sizes of circle shapes.
- **Language acquisition**—Discussing the circles created, such as their size, color, and placement on paper. For example, may begin using words such as "overlap" when circles are placed on top of each other.
- **Fine motor and hand-eye coordination skills**—Using and maneuvering the plunger to create a design.

Table 3.3 Literacy Skills Nurtured in the Plunger Print Experience

Visual Perception & Discrimination	Sequencing	Language Acquisition	Fine Motor	Gross Motor	Hand-Eye Coordination	Critical Thinking
●		●	●		●	

Art Experience 4: Circle Designs

Language Art Benchmarks:

Writing Standard 1(Level pre-K)

- Uses writing tools and materials (e.g., pencils, crayons, chalk, markers, rubber stamps, computers, paper, cardboard, chalkboard)

Listening and Speaking Standard 8 (Level Pre-K)

- Uses new vocabulary to describe feelings, thoughts, experiences, and observations
- Uses descriptive language (e.g., color words; size words, such as bigger, smaller; shape words)
- Follows one- and two-step directions

National Visual Arts Standards:

Understanding and Applying Media, Techniques, and Processes

- Knows the difference between materials and techniques
- Describes how different materials, techniques, and processes cause different responses
- Uses different media, techniques, and processes to communicate ideas, experiences, and stories
- Uses art materials and tools in a safe and responsible manner

Suggested Vocabulary Words:

Circles, repeat, overlap, larger, smaller

Materials Needed:

Reinforcement rings in assorted colors (used to reinforce punched holes on notebook paper)

Assorted colors of construction paper

Circle-shaped paper punches

Glue sticks

Black construction paper

Procedure:

1. Using a paper punch, punch out circles from a variety of colors of construction paper. Save the punched-out circles and the construction paper with the punched-out holes.
2. On black construction paper, glue punched-out circles and pieces of punched construction paper using a glue stick. Overlap papers for interesting effects.
3. Add to your creation gummed reinforcement rings in a variety of colors and sizes.
4. Encourage children to talk about their circle collages. Introduce vocabulary words, such as overlap, under, over.

Table 3.4 Literacy Skills Nurtured in the Circle Design Experience

Visual Perception & Discrimination	Sequencing	Language Acquisition	Fine Motor	Gross Motor	Hand-Eye Coordination	Critical Thinking
●		●	●		●	

What Children Will Learn:

- **Circle sizes and colors**—Using a variety to create an aesthetically pleasing composition.
- **Visual discrimination skills**—Observing the different colors and sizes of circles.
- **Language acquisition**—Discussing colors and sizes of circles used in their composition.
- **Fine motor and hand-eye coordination skills**—Securing each colored circle onto the paper.

Art Experience 5: Sand Drawing

Language Art Benchmarks:

Writing Standard 1(Level Pre-K)

- Knows that writing, including pictures, letters, and words, communicates meaning and information
- Uses writing tools and materials (e.g., pencils, crayons, chalk, markers, rubber stamps, computers, paper, cardboard, chalkboard)

Listening and Speaking Standard 8 (Level Pre-K)

- Uses new vocabulary to describe feelings, thoughts, experiences, and observations.
- Uses new vocabulary to describe feelings, thoughts, experiences, and observations
- Uses descriptive language (e.g., color words; size words, such as bigger, smaller; shape words)
- Follows one- and two-step directions

Listening and Speaking Standard 8 (Level 1)

- Uses level-appropriate vocabulary in speech (e.g., number words; words that describe people, places, things, events, location, actions; synonyms; antonyms; homonyms; word analogies; common figures of speech)
- Gives and responds to oral directions

Suggested Vocabulary Words:

Sand, gritty, rough, lines, pattern, repeat

Materials Needed:

Metal baking pan or cookie sheet with low edges

Construction paper in assorted colors to fit the bottom of the pan

Sand in assorted colors

Sand-drawing tools such as tongue depressors, Popsicle sticks, chopsticks

Procedure:

1. Line the bottom of the pan with construction paper. Glue into place.
2. Cover the paper with about 1/2 inch of sand in a color that contrasts with the paper. Try orange sand with blue paper, yellow sand with violet paper, green sand with red paper.
3. Gently shake the pan so that the sand covers the paper evenly.
4. Have the children feel or explore the sand before drawing.
5. Draw lines, curves, and words in the sand using fingers and tools.
6. Pat the designs with hands to smooth the sand and start again.
7. Talk with the children about how the sand feels and note the various line patterns they make.

National Visual Arts Standards:

Understanding and Applying Media, Techniques, and Processes

- Knows the difference between materials and techniques
- Describes how different materials, techniques, and processes cause different responses
- Uses different media, techniques, and processes to communicate ideas, experiences, and stories
- Uses art materials and tools in a safe and responsible manner

Using Knowledge of Structures and Functions

- Knows the differences among visual characteristics and purposes of art in order to convey ideas

Choosing and Evaluating a Range of Subject Matter, Symbols, and Ideas

- Selects and uses subject matter, symbols, and ideas to communicate meaning

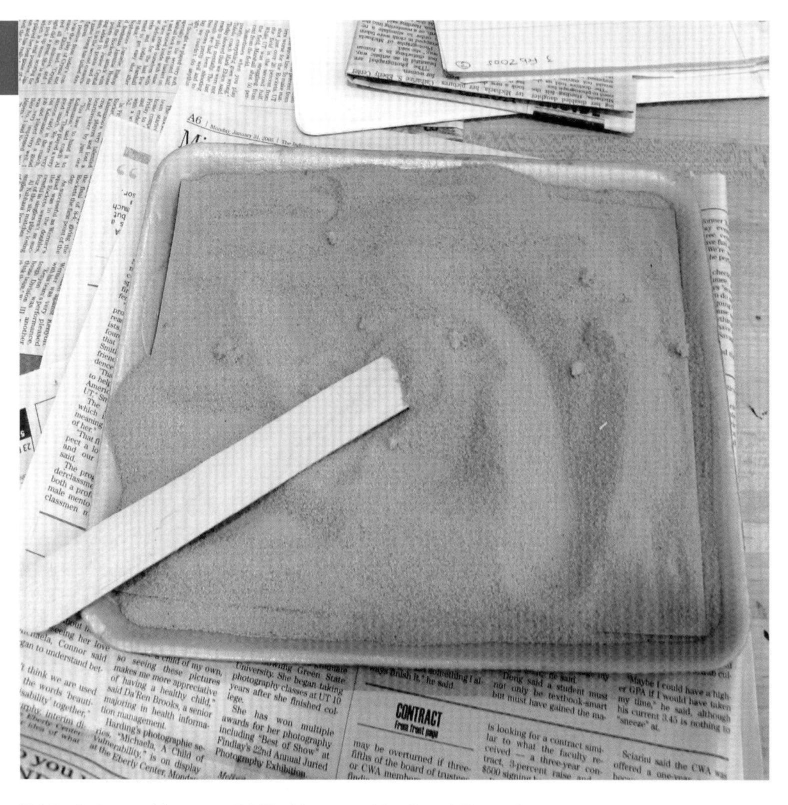

Table 3.5 Literacy Skills Nurtured in Sand Drawing

Visual Perception & Discrimination	Sequencing	Language Acquisition	Fine Motor	Gross Motor	Hand-Eye Coordination	Critical Thinking
●			●		●	

What Children Will Learn:

- **New sensory experience**— Drawing or writing on a different kind of surface (typically children draw on a light surface using a dark tool).
- **Visual discrimination skills**—Noticing the differences between materials and the markings they make in the sand.
- **Fine motor and hand-eye coordination skills**—Using their fingers or drawing tools to make markings in the sand.

Art Experience 6: Race Car Drawing

Language Art Benchmarks:

Writing Standard 1(Level pre-K)

- Uses writing tools and materials (e.g., pencils, crayons, chalk, markers, rubber stamps, computers, paper, cardboard, chalkboard)

Listening and Speaking Standard 8 (Level Pre-K)

- Uses new vocabulary to describe feelings, thoughts, experiences, and observations
- Uses descriptive language (e.g., color words; size words, such as bigger, smaller; shape words)
- Follows one- and two-step directions

Listening and Speaking Standard 8 (Level 1)

- Gives and responds to oral directions

National Visual Arts Standards:

Understanding and Applying Media, Techniques, and Processes

- Knows the difference between materials and techniques
- Describes how different materials, techniques, and processes cause different responses
- Uses different media, techniques, and processes to communicate ideas, experiences, and stories
- Uses art materials and tools in a safe and responsible manner

Suggested Vocabulary Words:

Race, drive, swerve, twist, forward, backward

Materials Needed:

Battery-operated race cars

Markers

Masking tape

Roll of white paper approximately 24 inches by 40 inches

Art Dog by Thatcher Hurd

Procedure:

1. Read *Art Dog* by Thatcher Hurd.
2. Talk about the different lines made by Art Dog's car.
3. Talk to the children about making their own lines with a remote-control car.
4. Choose two or three markers in colors of your choice.
5. Attach markers to the back and sides of the race car so that the tips of the markers (with caps off) touch the floor. Secure with masking tape.
6. Place a long sheet of white paper on the floor. Secure with tape.
7. Place car on the paper and operate with the remote control.
8. Tell children they can draw free-form scribbles or a picture, or try to write their name.

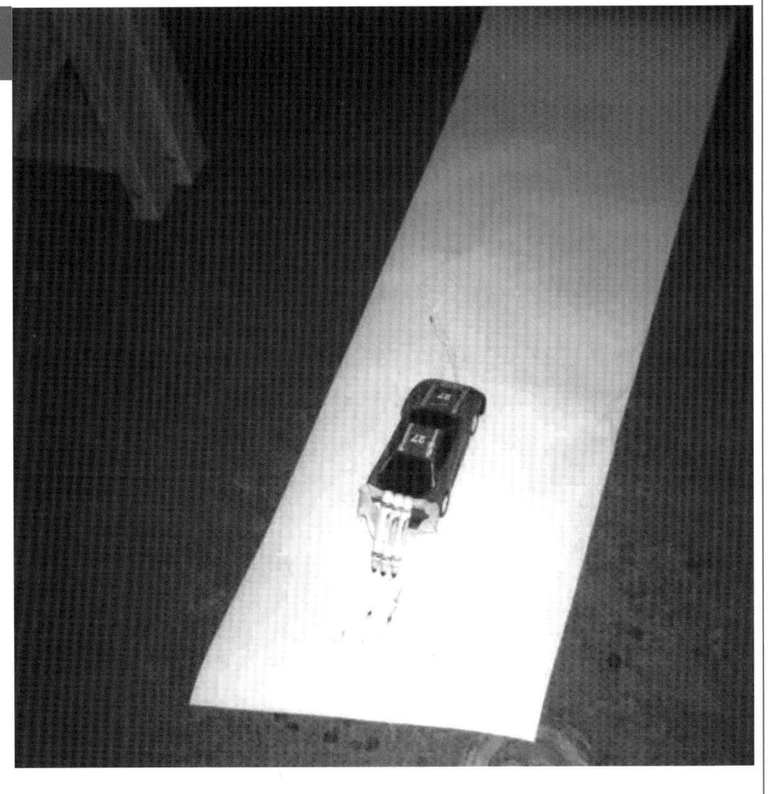

Table 3.6 Literacy Skills Nurtured in Race Car Drawing

Visual Perception & Discrimination	Sequencing	Language Acquisition	Fine Motor	Gross Motor	Hand-Eye Coordination	Critical Thinking
●			●		●	

What Children Will Learn:

- **Hand-eye coordination and fine motor skills**—Using the car controller to move the car, a skill that is similar to using a mouse to operate a computer.
- **Visual discrimination**—Tracking the car while steering, the same skill that is needed for reading text.

Art Experience 7: Styrofoam Prints

Language Art Benchmarks:

Writing Standard 1(Level Pre-K)

- Uses forms of emergent writing (e.g., scribble writing, random symbols, random letter-like marks) to represent ideas
- Uses writing tools and materials (e.g., pencils, crayons, chalk, markers, rubber stamps, computers, paper, cardboard, chalkboard)

Reading Standard 5 (Level Pre-K)

- Understands that illustrations and pictures convey meaning

Listening and Speaking Standard 8 (Level Pre-K)

- Uses new vocabulary to describe feelings, thoughts, experiences, and observations
- Uses descriptive language (e.g., color words; size words, such as bigger, smaller; shape words)
- Follows one- and two-step directions

Listening and Speaking Standard 8 (Level 1)

- Gives and responds to oral directions

National Visual Arts Standards:

Understanding and Applying Media, Techniques, and Processes

- Knows the difference between materials and techniques
- Describes how different materials, techniques, and processes cause different responses
- Uses different media, techniques, and processes to communicate ideas, experiences, and stories
- Uses art materials and tools in a safe and responsible manner

Choosing and Evaluating a Range of Subject Matter, Symbols, and Ideas

- Selects and uses subject matter, symbols, and ideas to communicate meaning

Materials Needed:

Styrofoam meat trays

Objects to make impressions such as keys, paper clips, coins

Water-base block printing inks in various colors

Brayer roller for applying ink

Piece of glass or Plexiglas

8-inch by 11-inch white drawing paper

Examples of woodblock prints made by various artists such as Hokusai and Hiroshige

Procedure:

1. Share woodblock prints with the children. Talk about how they were made and relate the process to the one they will be using to make Styrofoam prints.
2. Cut Styrofoam into a workable size (approximately 5 inches by 7 inches).
3. Using an assortment of objects, make impressions onto the entire surface of the Styrofoam. Encourage children to make a pattern in their impressions.
4. On a piece of Plexiglas, squeeze a small amount of block printing ink and spread evenly over the surface using a brayer.
5. Roll ink over the textured surface of the Styrofoam using the brayer.
6. Place a piece of paper on top of the inked surface and rub with the palm of your hand.
7. Pull the paper from the Styrofoam and you will have a print.
8. Repeat the process using different colors.

Suggested Vocabulary Words:

Styrofoam, print, ink, brayer

Table 3.7 Literacy Skills Nurtured in the Styrofoam Print Experience

Visual Perception & Discrimination	Sequencing	Language Acquisition	Fine Motor	Gross Motor	Hand-Eye Coordination	Critical Thinking
●		●	●		●	●

What Children Will Learn:

- **Cause and effect**—Engaging in the printing process.
- **Visual perception and discrimination, fine motor skills, and hand-eye coordination**—Creating linear patterns and textures by making impressions on the Styrofoam surface.
- **Language acquisition**—Conversing with an adult during the activity.
- **Critical thinking skills**—Finding appropriate language to describe the results of their work.

Art Experience 8: Colored-Water Tube Weaving

Language Art Benchmarks:

Reading Standard 5 (Level Pre-K)

- Understands that illustrations and pictures convey meaning

Listening and Speaking Standard 8 (Level Pre-K)

- Uses new vocabulary to describe feelings, thoughts, experiences, and observations
- Uses descriptive language (e.g., color words; size words, such as bigger, smaller; shape words)
- Follows one- and two-step directions

Listening and Speaking Standard 8 (Level 1)

- Gives and responds to oral directions

National Visual Arts Standards:

Understanding and Applying Media, Techniques, and Processes

- Knows the difference between materials and techniques
- Describes how different materials, techniques, and processes cause different responses
- Uses different media, techniques, and processes to communicate ideas, experiences, and stories
- Uses art materials and tools in a safe and responsible manner

Suggested Vocabulary Words:

Tube, weave, gravity, blend, chase, funnel, pitcher

Materials Needed:

Plastic funnel
Clear plastic tubing
Duct tape
Food coloring
Small plastic cups and pitchers of water
Plastic mesh fencing used in construction or landscaping
Bucket

Procedure:

1. Cut fencing material to fit a large window frame.
2. Using duct tape, adhere mesh fencing material to the window frame.
3. Weave the plastic tubing into the mesh in any desired way, making sure that the end of the tube is at the bottom with a bucket underneath.
4. Insert the funnel into the top end of the clear plastic tubing, making sure that it is snug.
5. Mix food coloring and water into pitchers, one color per pitcher.
6. Pour the colored water into separate cups.
7. Pour each cup of water into the funnel and watch it travel down the clear tube.
8. Add a different color and watch the two colors mix in the tube.
9. Continue to add a variety of colors and watch the effects.
10. Talk to the children about the colors that mix as they travel down the tube. This is a great opportunity for children to learn about the concept of gravity.

Table 3.8 Literacy Skills Nurtured in Color Tube Weaving

Visual Perception & Discrimination	Sequencing	Language Acquisition	Fine Motor	Gross Motor	Hand-Eye Coordination	Critical Thinking
●	●	●	●		●	●

What Children Will Learn:

- **Visual discrimination, fine motor, and hand-eye coordination skills**—Weaving of materials.
- **Sequencing**—Following the procedure step by step to successfully complete this activity.
- **Critical thinking**—Deciding how to weave the tubes for the water to flow.
- **Language and vocabulary**—Talking about how the colors are mixing and how the water is flowing.

Art Experience 9: Boats

Language Art Benchmarks:

Reading Standard 5 (Level Pre-K)

- Understands that illustrations and pictures convey meaning

Listening and Speaking Standard 8 (Level Pre-K)

- Uses new vocabulary to describe feelings, thoughts, experiences, and observations
- Uses descriptive language (e.g., color words; size words, such as bigger, smaller; shape words)
- Follows one- and two-step directions

Listening and Speaking Standard 8 (Level 1)

- Gives and responds to oral directions

National Visual Arts Standards:

Understanding and Applying Media, Techniques, and Processes

- Knows the difference between materials and techniques
- Describes how different materials, techniques, and processes cause different responses
- Uses different media, techniques, and processes to communicate ideas, experiences, and stories
- Uses art materials and tools in a safe and responsible manner

Suggested Vocabulary Words:

Boat, float, sink, light, heavy, sail

Materials Needed:

Scissors
Glue
Glue guns
Pipe cleaners
Styrofoam pieces
Cardboard scraps
Wood scraps
Paper scraps
Assorted found and recycled materials

Procedure:

1. Look at a variety of paintings of boats by artists such as Homer, Monet, Van Gogh. Discuss the similarities and differences. Pose questions such as: How do boats float? What materials are used to build them? How do sails help boats to float better?
2. Read books about boats, such as *Jennifer's Rabbit* by Tom Paxton.
3. Listen to music inspired by the sea, such as *Echoes of Nature: Ocean Waves* by Kim Wilson.
4. Divide children into groups and tell them they are to build a boat out of recycled and found materials. They must make a boat that floats.
5. As they work, play music inspired by the sea.
6. After the boats are completed, have children test their boats to see if they will float by putting them into a small swimming pool or water table.
7. Simulate storm conditions by blowing a fan over the water to make ripples. Have the children decide on other ways to create their own storm at sea.
8. Encourage children to tell stories about their boats.

Table 3.9 Literacy Skills Nurtured in the Boat-making Experience

Visual Perception & Discrimination	Sequencing	Language Acquisition	Fine Motor	Gross Motor	Hand-Eye Coordination	Critical Thinking
●	●	●	●		●	●

What Children Will Learn:

- **Critical thinking, problem solving, and language acquisition skills**—Constructing a boat that floats.
- **Social skills**—Working collaboratively with other children.
- **Visual discrimination, hand-eye, and fine motor skills**—Selecting appropriate materials and constructing their boat.
- **Sequencing and vocabulary skills**—Telling a story about their boat.

Art Experience 10: Fruit and Veggies on a Light Table

Language Art Benchmarks:

Listening and Speaking Standard 8 (Level Pre-K)

- Uses new vocabulary to describe feelings, thoughts, experiences, and observations
- Uses descriptive language (e.g., color words; size words, such as bigger, smaller; shape words)
- Follows one- and two-step directions

Listening and Speaking Standard 8 (Level 1)

- Gives and responds to oral directions

National Visual Arts Standards:

Understanding and Applying Media, Techniques, and Processes

- Knows the difference between materials and techniques
- Describes how different materials, techniques, and processes cause different responses
- Uses art materials and tools in a safe and responsible manner

Suggested Vocabulary Words:

Fruit, pattern, repeat, overlap, transparent

Materials Needed:

An assortment of fruits and vegetables sliced thick (such as oranges, lemons and limes, star fruit, onions)

Light table

Books on fruit and vegetables such as *Planting a Rainbow* or *Market Day* by Lois Ehlert

Artworks of fruit

Procedure:

1. Place sliced fruits and vegetables on the light table.
2. Invite children to make patterns with the fruit.
3. Allow children to explore the fruits and vegetables more closely by using a magnifying glass.
4. Read books on fruits and vegetables.

What Children Will Learn:

- **The properties of different fruits and vegetables.**
- **Vocabulary**—Listening to the adult use descriptive language.
- **Visual discrimination, fine motor, and hand-eye coordination skills**—Picking up each slice of fruit or vegetable and placing them the light table.
- **Sequencing and critical thinking skills**—Planning out a pattern with the fruit.

Table 3.10 Literacy Skills Nurtured in the Fruit on Light Table Experience

Visual Perception & Discrimination	Sequencing	Language Acquisition	Fine Motor	Gross Motor	Hand-Eye Coordination	Critical Thinking
●	●	●	●		●	●

Art Experience 11: Sandpaper Prints

Language Art Benchmarks:

Writing Standard 1 (Level Pre-K)

- Uses forms of emergent writing (e.g., scribble writing, random symbols, random letter-like marks) to represent ideas
- Uses writing tools and materials (e.g., pencils, crayons, chalk, markers, rubber stamps, computers, paper, cardboard, chalkboard)

Reading Standard 5 (Level Pre-K)

- Understands that illustrations and pictures convey meaning

Listening and Speaking Standard 8 (Level Pre-K)

- Uses new vocabulary to describe feelings, thoughts, experiences, and observations
- Uses descriptive language (e.g., color words; size words, such as bigger, smaller; shape words)
- Follows one- and two-step directions

Listening and Speaking Standard 8 (Level 1)

- Gives and responds to oral directions

National Visual Arts Standards:

Understanding and Applying Media, Techniques, and Processes

- Knows the difference between materials and techniques
- Describes how different materials, techniques, and processes cause different responses
- Uses different media, techniques, and processes to communicate ideas, experiences, and stories
- Uses art materials and tools in a safe and responsible manner

Choosing and Evaluating a Range of Subject Matter, Symbols, and Ideas

- Selects and uses subject matter, symbols, and ideas to communicate meaning

Materials Needed:

5-inch by 7-inch pieces of medium-grade sand paper

Crayons

9-inch by 12-inch manila paper

Iron

Newspaper

Works by Impressionists, such as Monet, Seurat, Renoir

Procedure:

1. Have the children draw on sandpaper using a crayon. Encourage them to press hard to get good coverage.
2. Set iron on "cotton" setting. Teachers should assist as necessary to be sure children don't burn themselves.
3. Make a padding with newspaper.
4. After the iron is heated, place the sandpaper, drawing side facing up, onto the newspaper.
5. Place a piece of manila paper on top.
6. Iron the paper.
7. The crayon will melt onto the paper, leaving a "pebbly" effect.
8. Talk to the children about the texture. Have them describe to you what it looks like.
9. Have children view artworks by the Impressionists. How does their work compare?

Suggested Vocabulary Words:

Sandpaper, texture, rough, transfer, print, iron

Table 3.11 Literacy Skills Nurtured in Sand Paper Print Experience

Visual Perception & Discrimination	Sequencing	Language Acquisition	Fine Motor	Gross Motor	Hand-Eye Coordination	Critical Thinking
		●	●		●	

What Children Will Learn:

- **Cause and effect**—Discovering how the melted crayon drawing changes when transferred to paper.
- **Vocabulary**—Describing their work and comparing it to other artists.
- **Fine motor and hand-eye coordination skills**—Executing their drawings onto the sand paper.

Art Experience 12: Hats

Language Art Benchmarks:

Reading Standard 5 (Level Pre-K)

- Understands that illustrations and pictures convey meaning

Listening and Speaking Standard 8 (Level Pre-K)

- Uses new vocabulary to describe feelings, thoughts, experiences, and observations
- Uses descriptive language (e.g., color words; size words, such as bigger, smaller; shape words)
- Follows one- and two-step directions

Listening and Speaking Standard 8 (Level 1)

- Gives and responds to oral directions

National Visual Arts Standards:

Understanding and Applying Media, Techniques, and Processes

- Knows the difference between materials and techniques
- Describes how different materials, techniques, and processes cause different responses
- Uses different media, techniques, and processes to communicate ideas, experiences, and stories
- Uses art materials and tools in a safe and responsible manner

Choosing and Evaluating a Range of Subject Matter, Symbols, and Ideas

- Selects and uses subject matter, symbols, and ideas to communicate meaning

Suggested Vocabulary Words:

Hat, fit, head, scrunch, tape

Procedure:

1. Cover work area with newspaper.
2. Look at paintings of people wearing different hats.
3. Read the story *Jenny's Hat* by Ezra Jack Keats.
4. Look at the book *Hats, Hats, Hats* by Ann Morris. Talk about all of the different hats that people wear during different seasons, in different cultures, and in various professions.
5. Spread out one piece of newspaper and cover it with liquid white glue.
6. Place another sheet of newspaper on top and cover it with glue.
7. Repeat this layering of newspaper four times.
8. Have a partner place the damp newspaper on your head.
9. Have a partner use masking tape to form the paper on the crown of your head and wrap the masking tape around to hold it into place.
10. Take off the newspaper and shape it.
11. The brim of this hat form can be cut into any length and shaped. Use shorter brims for "baseball" style caps and longer brims for a "sombrero" style hat.
12. Let it dry overnight.
13. When dry, the hat can be painted with any colors. Use more than one coat to have good coverage.
14. Let it dry overnight.
15. Decorate the hat with feathers, buttons, lace, etc.
16. Have a fashion show to display the hats.
17. Encourage dramatic play as each child becomes a new character when wearing his or her hat.

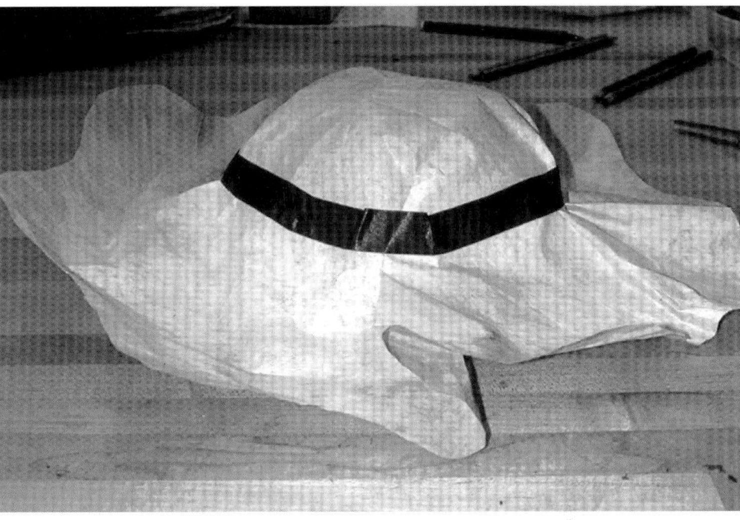

Table 3.12 Literacy Skills Nurtured in the Hat—Making Experience

Visual Perception & Discrimination	Sequencing	Language Acquisition	Fine Motor	Gross Motor	Hand-Eye Coordination	Critical Thinking
		●	●		●	●

Materials Needed:

Paintings of people wearing different kinds of hats

Picture books on hats: *Jenny's Hat* by Ezra Jack Keats; *Hats, Hats, Hats* by Ann Morris

Newspaper

Liquid white glue

Tempera paints

Brushes in assorted sizes

Feathers, ribbons, glitter, pipe cleaners, buttons, lace, etc.

Assorted colors of masking tape

What Children Will Learn:

- **Critical thinking skills**—Viewing and comparing paintings and books showing people wearing hats.
- **Vocabulary**—Discussing various hats and reasons for wearing them.
- **Fine motor and hand-eye coordination**—Constructing and shaping a hat out of newspaper.
- **Language acquisition**—Engaging in dramatic play.

Art Experience 13: Letters in a Tube

Language Art Benchmarks:

Writing Standard 1 (Level Pre-K)

- Uses knowledge of letters to write or copy familiar words, such as own name

Listening and Speaking Standard 8 (Level Pre-K)

- Uses new vocabulary to describe feelings, thoughts, experiences, and observations
- Uses descriptive language (e.g., color words; size words, such as bigger, smaller; shape words)
- Follows one- and two-step directions

Listening and Speaking Standard 8 (Level 1)

- Gives and responds to oral directions

National Visual Arts Standards:

Understanding and Applying Media, Techniques, and Processes

- Knows the difference between materials and techniques
- Describes how different materials, techniques, and processes cause different responses
- Uses different media, techniques, and processes to communicate ideas, experiences, and stories
- Uses art materials and tools in a safe and responsible manner

Suggested Vocabulary Words:

Use words from your classroom's vocabulary or spelling list

Materials Needed:

Small clear plastic water bottles with labels removed

Water (regular and seltzer)

Baby oil

Liquid watercolors

Glitter

Alphabet noodle letters (may be purchased at most grocery store pasta sections)

Procedure:

1. Have small groups of children choose a word. This word can be from the current spelling list or vocabulary words that have been discussed in your class. You might provide a word bank for children to choose from.
2. Once a word is selected, tell children it is "top secret." They are not to share it with children in other groups.
3. Have groups place the letters of their word in an empty clear plastic water bottle.
4. Fill the water bottle with water (regular or seltzer).
5. Add a drop of liquid water color.
6. Add oil and glitter, if desired.
7. When complete, put the lid tightly on the bottle.
8. Ask groups of children to swap their bottles for a different one.
9. Each group has to guess what the word is in their bottle.
10. Have children write each letter on paper. They will then have to unscramble the letters to figure out the word.
11. When complete, have groups share their word with the class.

Table 3.13 Literacy Skills Nurtured in the Letters in a Tube Experience

Visual Perception & Discrimination	Sequencing	Language Acquisition	Fine Motor	Gross Motor	Hand-Eye Coordination	Critical Thinking
●		●	●		●	●

What Children Will Learn:

- **Vocabulary**—Unscrambling letters to make words.
- **Critical thinking and problem-solving skills**—Guessing the word in the bottle.
- **Fine motor and hand-eye coordination skills**—Placing letter noodles into the bottle.

Art Experience 14: Model Magic Bottle Cap Prints

Language Art Benchmarks:

Writing Standard 1 (Level Pre-K)

- Uses knowledge of letters to write or copy familiar words, such as own name

Listening and Speaking Standard 8 (Level Pre-K)

- Uses new vocabulary to describe feelings, thoughts, experiences, and observations
- Uses descriptive language (e.g., color words; size words, such as bigger, smaller; shape words)
- Follows one- and two-step directions

Listening and Speaking Standard 8 (Level 1)

- Gives and responds to oral directions

National Visual Arts Standards:

Understanding and Applying Media, Techniques, and Processes

- Knows the difference between materials and techniques
- Describes how different materials, techniques, and processes cause different responses
- Uses different media, techniques, and processes to communicate ideas, experiences, and stories
- Uses art materials and tools in a safe and responsible manner

Choosing and Evaluating a Range of Subject Matter, Symbols, and Ideas

- Selects and uses subject matter, symbols, and ideas to communicate meaning

Suggested Vocabulary Words:

Print, texture, press, ink

Materials Needed:

Recycled plastic bottle caps

Model Magic (modeling compound made by Crayola®)

Ink stamp pads in a variety of colors

Pencils or pens

Manila paper

Newspaper

Various examples of printed fabrics such as Adinkra cloth

Procedure:

1. Cover work area with newspaper.
2. Provide each child with a bottle cap and a small amount of Model Magic.
3. Have each child press the Model Magic inside the cap until it rises slightly above the ridge of the cap.
4. Have the child use a pencil, pen, or other object to press a pattern into the Model Magic.
5. Let Model Magic dry overnight.
6. When dry and hardened, press the Model Magic stamper into an ink pad and press onto a piece of manila paper to make a print. Repeat this step to make a pattern.
7. Encourage children to share stampers and explore various designs.
8. Encourage them to discuss their explorations and discoveries.
9. Look at various printed textile designs with the children. Have them compare their patterns with those on the cloth. How are they the same? How are they different?

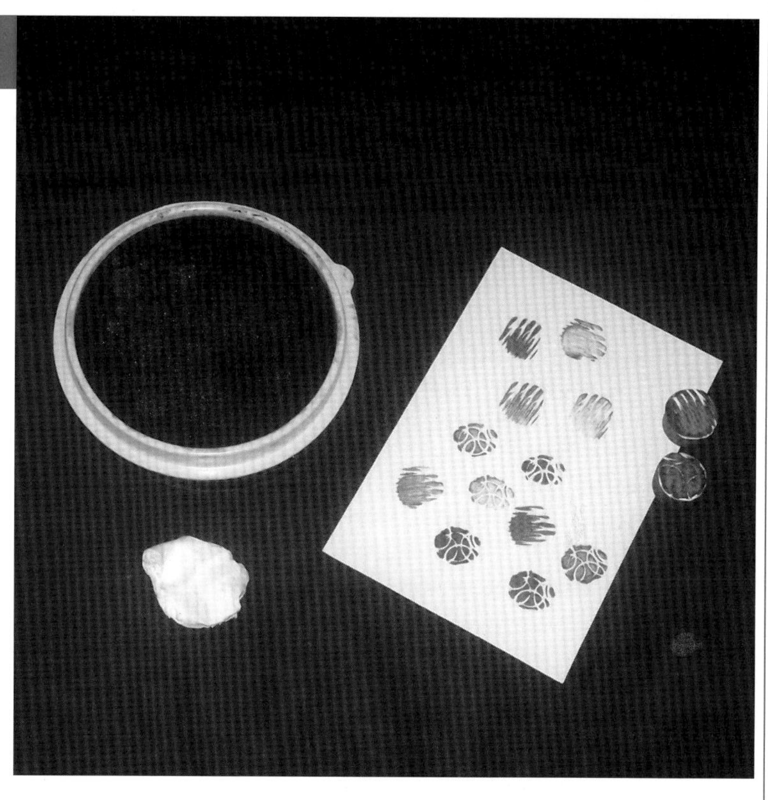

Table 3.14 Literacy Skills Nurtured in Bottle Cap Print Experience

Visual Perception & Discrimination	Sequencing	Language Acquisition	Fine Motor	Gross Motor	Hand-Eye Coordination	Critical Thinking
●	●	●	●		●	

What Children Will Learn:

- **Fine motor, hand-eye coordination, and visual discrimination skills**—Making stampers.
- **Sequencing**—Making patterns with stampers.
- **Language skills**—Talking about their discoveries in making patterns.

Art Experience 15: Starry Night

Language Art Benchmarks:

Writing Standard 1 (Level Pre-K)

- Uses writing tools and materials (e.g., pencils, crayons, chalk, markers, rubber stamps, computers, paper, cardboard, chalkboard)

Listening and Speaking Standard 8 (Level Pre-K)

- Uses new vocabulary to describe feelings, thoughts, experiences, and observations
- Uses descriptive language (e.g., color words; size words, such as bigger, smaller; shape words)
- Follows one- and two-step directions

Listening and Speaking Standard 8 (Level 1)

- Gives and responds to oral directions

National Visual Arts Standards:

Understanding and Applying Media, Techniques, and Processes

- Knows the difference between materials and techniques
- Describes how different materials, techniques, and processes cause different responses
- Uses different media, techniques, and processes to communicate ideas, experiences, and stories
- Uses art materials and tools in a safe and responsible manner

Choosing and Evaluating a Range of Subject Matter, Symbols, and Ideas

- Selects and uses subject matter, symbols, and ideas to communicate meaning

Suggested Vocabulary Words:

Texture, swirl, paint, thick, thin

Materials Needed:

8 ½-inch by 11-inch white tagboard

Thick tempera paints or puff paints (red, blue, yellow, white, and black)

1-inch sponge-tip brush

Tools to make textures (for example; toothbrushes, forks, toothpicks, and combs)

Newspaper

Paper plates

Glow-in-the-dark stars

Art reproduction of *Starry Night* by Vincent Van Gogh

Procedure:

1. Look at a painting reproduction of *Starry Night* by Vincent Van Gogh. Talk about the night sky and the way that it looks when all the stars can be seen.
2. Read the story *The First Starry Night* by Joan Shaddox Isom
3. Place tagboard on a newspaper-covered area and have children paint a night sky using thick tempera paints and a sponge-tip brush. Encourage the mixing of new colors using a paper plate palette. Talk about the colors of the night sky.
4. Using a variety of tools, create a texture in the sky by scraping the tools across the thick paint.
5. While paint is still wet, place glow-in-the-dark stars in desired locations. Or glue stars after the paint has dried.
6. While children are working, play Don McLean's "Vincent," a song about Vincent Van Gogh.
7. When paintings are dry, turn off the lights to view the glow-in-the-dark stars.
8. Talk with children about looking at the stars at night.

Table 3.15 Literacy Skills Nurtured in the Starry Night Experience

Visual Perception & Discrimination	Sequencing	Language Acquisition	Fine Motor	Gross Motor	Hand-Eye Coordination	Critical Thinking
●		●	●			

What Children Will Learn:

- **Fine motor and visual discrimination skills**—Mixing colors and creating textures with different tools.
- **Vocabulary**—Learning new words as adult describes the different textured lines made in each child's painting and talks about the night sky.

Art Experience 16: Illuminated Manuscripts

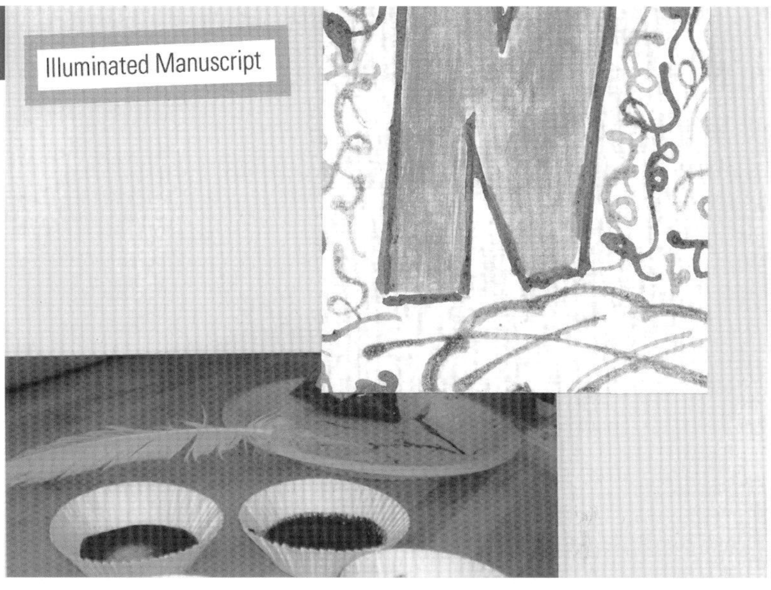

Language Art Benchmarks:

Writing Standard 1 (Level Pre-K)

- Knows that writing, including pictures, letters, and words, communicates meaning and information
- Uses drawings to express thoughts, feelings, and ideas
- Uses forms of emergent writing (e.g., scribble writing, random symbols, random letter-like marks) to represent ideas
- Uses emergent writing skills to write for a variety of purposes (e.g., to make lists, to send messages, to write stories) and to write in a variety of forms (e.g., journals, sign-in sheets, name cards, cards with words and pictures)
- Uses knowledge of letters to write or copy familiar words, such as own name
- Uses writing tools and materials (e.g., pencils, crayons, chalk, markers, rubber stamps, computers, paper, cardboard, chalkboard)

Writing Standard 1 (Level 1)

- Writes for different purposes (e.g., to entertain, inform, learn, communicate ideas

Suggested Vocabulary Words:

Illuminated manuscript, quill pen, ink, mortar, pestle

In the eighth century A.D., literacy was rare. King Charlemagne thought it was important that people under his reign could read and write. To this end, Charlemagne brought in scholars from all over the world. During this period of growth, Charlemagne developed a handwriting style that was eventually used throughout Europe. Monks in monasteries wrote in this style and copied the classics for the people to read. These works were illuminated by artists. Illuminations are hand-painted illustrations that decorate the first letter of a word, or are placed within the text or on the border of the page. Some of these illustrations are very elaborate and have been preserved so that they can still be seen in museums today.

Materials Needed:

Quill pens (with feathers purchased in a craft store)

Parchment paper, handmade inks, mortar and pestle, dried beet root, parsley, and saffron

Small containers for ink

Gold tempera paint

Procedure:

1. Share with students examples of illuminated manuscripts.
2. Read the story *Marguerite Makes a Book* by Bruce Robertson.
3. Have children make their own illuminated manuscripts by using quill pens and hand-made inks. Possible materials for inks are saffron, parsley, beet root, and charcoal. Place each item in a mortar and grind into a fine powder with a pestle. Add a small amount of water and beaten egg white (use pasteurized eggs) to the pigment. Mix it until the powder is dissolved.
4. Have children dip the tip of their quill pen into the ink and draw their illuminated manuscript on parchment. They can draw the first letter of their name or any letter of their choice.
5. When done, children can share their manuscripts and talk about them.

Table 3.16 Literacy Skills Nurtured in the Illuminated Manuscript Experience

Visual Perception & Discrimination	Sequencing	Language Acquisition	Fine Motor	Gross Motor	Hand-Eye Coordination	Critical Thinking
●		●	●		●	●

What Children Will Learn:

- **Visual discrimination, fine motor, and hand-eye coordination skills**—Drawing an illuminated manuscript.
- **Critical thinking**—Mixing the ingredients to make the ink; painting the letter.

National Visual Arts Standards:

Using Knowledge of Structures and Functions

- Know the differences among visual characteristics and purposes of art in order to convey ideas
- Describe how different expressive features and organizational principles cause different responses
- Use visual structures and functions of art to communicate ideas

Choosing and Evaluating a Range of Subject Matter, Symbols, and Ideas

- Explore and understand prospective content for works of art
- Select and use subject matter, symbols, and ideas to communicate meaning
- Know the visual arts have both a history and specific relationships to various cultures

Art Experience 17: Stone Designs

Language Art Benchmarks:

Listening and Speaking Standard 8 (Level Pre-K)

- Uses new vocabulary to describe feelings, thoughts, experiences, and observations
- Uses descriptive language (e.g., color words; size words, such as bigger, smaller; shape words)

National Visual Arts Standards:

Understanding and Applying Media, Techniques, and Processes

- Knows the difference between materials and techniques
- Describes how different materials, techniques, and processes cause different responses
- Uses different media, techniques, and processes to communicate ideas, experiences, and stories
- Uses art materials and tools in a safe and responsible manner

Suggested Vocabulary Words:

Pattern, design, repeat, small, large, spiral, zigzag, straight, curved

Materials Needed:

A variety of stones

Black paper (construction paper, roofing paper, or fabric)

Reproductions of artwork by Andy Goldsworthy

Procedure:

1. Look at nature art by Andy Goldsworthy, in particular, his stone designs.
2. Go on a nature walk and have children collect stones.
3. Place a large piece of paper on the floor and have children make linear patterns (such as spirals, straight lines, zigzags) with the stones.
4. Keep this stone design area in the classroom where children are free to make changes to the patterns whenever they wish.
5. Talk with the children about the patterns they have made.

Alternative:

Make stone patterns by pushing stones into Play-Doh (in earth colors) that has been pressed into a small box. This way, each child will have his or her own stone design to keep.

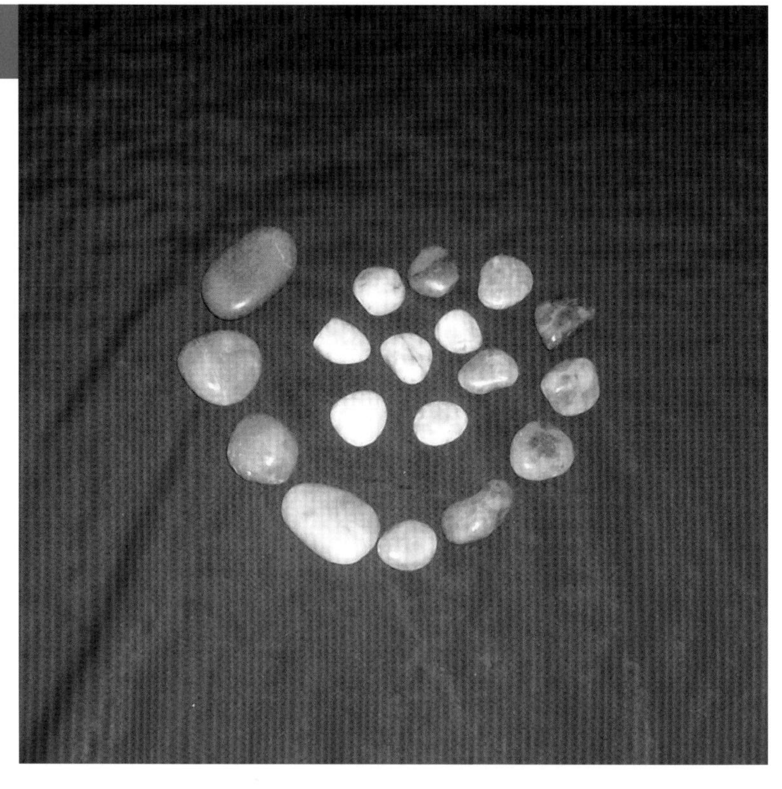

Table 3.17 Literacy Skills Nurtured in the Stone Design Experience

Visual Perception & Discrimination	Sequencing	Language Acquisition	Fine Motor	Gross Motor	Hand-Eye Coordination	Critical Thinking
●	●	●	●		●	●

What Children Will Learn:

- **Hand-eye coordination and visual perception and discrimination skills**—Choosing stones to make a pattern.
- **Sequencing and critical thinking skills**—Creating a stone pattern.
- **Language skills**—Talking about their completed work.

Art Experience 18: Marbleized Paper

Language Art Benchmarks:

Listening and Speaking Standard 8 (Level Pre-K)

- Speaks clearly enough to be understood by unfamiliar adults and uses appropriate levels of volume, tone, and inflection
- Uses new vocabulary to describe feelings, thoughts, experiences, and observations
- Uses descriptive language (e.g., color words; size words, such as bigger, smaller; shape words)
- Asks questions to obtain information
- Answers simple questions
- Follows conversation rules (e.g., taking turns, making relevant comments; staying on topic) when talking with peers and adults
- Listens for a variety of purposes (e.g., to gain and share information, to perform a task, for enjoyment, to learn what happened in a story, to converse with an adult or peer)
- Understands messages in conversations (e.g. responds differently based on purpose of messages in conversation; attends and responds to conversations)
- Follows one- and two-step directions

Suggested Vocabulary Words:

Print, marbleized, comb, swirl

Materials Needed:

Shaving cream
Assorted liquid food colors or watercolors
Plastic or Styrofoam trays
Combs
Cardboard
Scissors
Newspaper
8-inch by 10-inch white drawing paper

Procedure:

1. Cover work area with newspaper.
2. Place tray on top of newspaper and fill with shaving cream.
3. Place drops of food coloring or liquid watercolors randomly over shaving cream.
4. Using a comb, swirl colors together.
5. Place a sheet of white drawing paper on top of the shaving cream and lightly press.
6. Pull off the paper and scrape off excess shaving cream using a small piece of sturdy cardboard.
7. As the shaving cream is scraped off, the watercolor residue will leave a marbleized print.
8. Discuss with the child the new colors made, and the fragrance and texture of the shaving cream.

Safety note:

The shaving cream's fragrance may trigger an asthma attack. If possible, use unscented shaving cream.

Table 3.18 Literacy Skills Nurtured in the Marbleized Paper Experience

Visual Perception & Discrimination	Sequencing	Language Acquisition	Fine Motor	Gross Motor	Hand-Eye Coordination	Critical Thinking
●	●	●	●		●	

What Children Will Learn:

- **Color mixing.**
- **Visual discrimination, fine motor, and hand-eye coordination skills**—Handling the materials and exploring various color combinations.
- **Sequencing skills**—Following the steps to make a piece of marbleized paper.
- **Language development**—Discussing the steps and the results of color explorations.

Art Experience 19: Color Mixing Experimentation

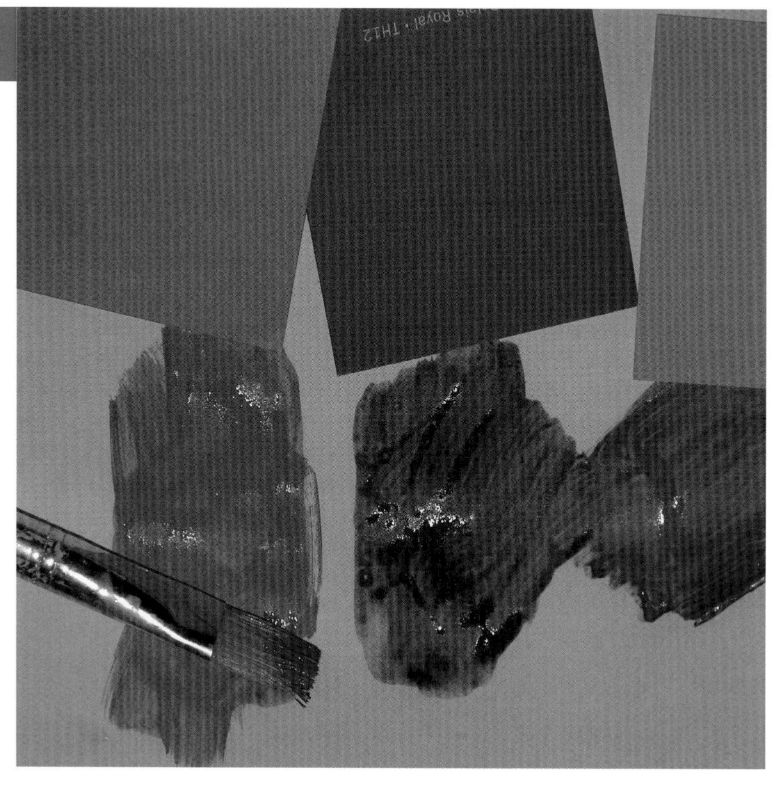

Language Art Benchmarks:

Listening and Speaking Standard 8 (Level Pre-K)

- Speaks clearly enough to be understood by unfamiliar adults and uses appropriate levels of volume, tone, and inflection
- Uses new vocabulary to describe feelings, thoughts, experiences, and observations
- Uses descriptive language (e.g., color words; size words, such as bigger, smaller; shape words)
- Asks questions to obtain information
- Answers simple questions
- Follows conversation rules (e.g., taking turns, making relevant comments; staying on topic) when talking with peers and adults
- Listens for a variety of purposes (e.g., to gain and share information, to perform a task, for enjoyment, to learn what happened in a story, to converse with an adult or peer)
- Understands messages in conversations (e.g. responds differently based on purpose of messages in conversation; attends and responds to conversations)
- Follows one- and two-step directions

Suggested Vocabulary Words:

Mix, blend, create, proportion, measuring terms (tablespoon, teaspoon, etc.)

Materials Needed:

Newspaper

Paper plates

Assorted paintbrushes

Red, yellow, blue, white, and black tempera paint

Paint-color samples from hardware store or paint store

Procedure:

1. Cover work area with newspaper.
2. Place all five colors of tempera paint onto a paper plate and place on top of the newspaper.
3. Place additional empty paper plates in the work area.
4. Have children work in small groups. Give each group a paint sample. Ask them to mix their tempera paints to make the color given to them.
5. Give children as much time as they need to experiment with color mixing.
6. Encourage conversation among the children in each group while asking open-ended questions that will help them in this exploratory exercise.

Table 3.19 Literacy Skills Nurtured in Color Mixing

Visual Perception & Discrimination	Sequencing	Language Acquisition	Fine Motor	Gross Motor	Hand-Eye Coordination	Critical Thinking
●		●	●		●	●

What Children Will Learn:

- **Problem solving**—Staying focused until the answer is found.
- **Critical thinking skills**—Figuring out what color combinations are needed to make a new color and matching it to the color swatch they were given.
- **Language and social skills**—Collaborating on solving this problem together.
- **Visual discrimination**—Carefully matching the color they are making with the color swatch they were given.
- **Fine motor and hand-eye coordination skills**—Mixing new colors using a paintbrush.
- **Vocabulary**—Talking as they work as a group to solve the problem.

Art Experience 20: Colored Pegs on a Light Table

Language Art Benchmarks:

Listening and Speaking Standard 8 (Level Pre-K)

- Speaks clearly enough to be understood by unfamiliar adults and uses appropriate levels of volume, tone, and inflection
- Uses new vocabulary to describe feelings, thoughts, experiences, and observations
- Uses descriptive language (e.g., color words; size words, such as bigger, smaller; shape words)
- Asks questions to obtain information
- Answers simple questions
- Listens for a variety of purposes (e.g., to gain and share information, to perform a task, for enjoyment, to learn what happened in a story, to converse with an adult or peer)
- Understands messages in conversations (e.g. responds differently based on purpose of messages in conversation; attends and responds to conversations)
- Follows one- and two-step directions

Suggested Vocabulary Words:

Pattern, repeat, design, vertical, horizontal, diagonal

Materials Needed:

Light table

Small colored transparent pegs (such as the ones used for Lite-Brite)

Pegboard painted black (sized to fit over light table top)

Procedure:

1. Place black pegboard over light-table top.
2. Turn on light table.
3. Using the assorted colored pegs, have the child create a pattern by sequencing colors.
4. As they make their design, talk to them about color choices and introduce new vocabulary words.

What Children Will Learn:

- **Hand-eye coordination, fine motor and critical thinking skills**—Selecting colored pegs to make a pattern picture.
- **Sequencing skills**—Making the design.
- **Language skills**—Talking about the patterns and colors.

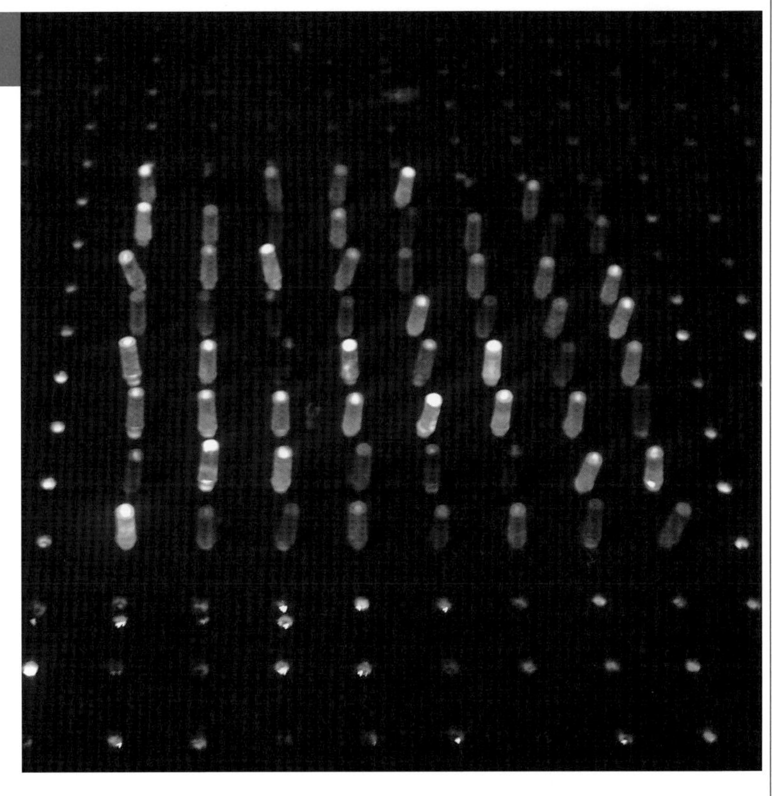

Table 3.20 Literacy Skills Nurtured in Colored Pegs Activity

Visual Perception & Discrimination	Sequencing	Language Acquisition	Fine Motor	Gross Motor	Hand-Eye Coordination	Critical Thinking
	●	●	●		●	●

Art Experience 21: Snowflakes on a Light Table

Language Art Benchmarks:

Listening and Speaking Standard 8 (Level Pre-K)

- Speaks clearly enough to be understood by unfamiliar adults and uses appropriate levels of volume, tone, and inflection
- Uses new vocabulary to describe feelings, thoughts, experiences, and observations
- Uses descriptive language (e.g., color words; size words, such as bigger, smaller; shape words)
- Asks questions to obtain information
- Answers simple questions
- Follows conversation rules (e.g., taking turns, making relevant comments; staying on topic) when talking with peers and adults
- Listens for a variety of purposes (e.g., to gain and share information, to perform a task, for enjoyment, to learn what happened in a story, to converse with an adult or peer)
- Understands messages in conversations (e.g. responds differently based on purpose of messages in conversation; attends and responds to conversations)

Suggested Vocabulary Words:

Snowflake, crystal, frozen, ice, weather

Materials Needed:

Light table

Blue cellophane

Assorted kinds of snowflakes (such as paper, plastic, holiday ornaments)

Books about snow

Paintings of snow scenes

Magic Nuddle®

Procedure:

1. On the wall behind the light table, hang a painting reproduction of a snow scene, such as *Winter Scene on a Canal* by Hendrick Avercamp.
2. Cover the light table with blue cellophane paper.
3. Look for a variety of snowflakes to place on the blue cellophane, such as die-cut vellum snowflakes, plastic snowflakes, holiday ornament snowflakes, etc.
4. Arrange the various snowflakes into different patterns.
5. Place books about snow and snowflakes near the light table for children to enjoy, such as: *Snow* by Uri Shulevitz, *The Snowy Day* by Ezra Jack Keats, *Dream Snow* by Eric Carle, and *The Little Book of Snowflakes* by Kenneth Libbrecht.
6. Listen to music, such as *Northern Lights: Music of Contemplation for a New Age.*
7. Ask children to explore the different kinds of snowflakes. Have them compare the paper and plastic snowflakes with the ones found in *The Little Book of Snowflakes.*
8. Look at the painting *Winter Scene on a Canal* by Hendrick Avercamp. Talk with the children about winter. Discuss the clothing that is worn by the people in the painting. Ask the children to tell you what else they can see in the painting. How does it feel to be in the snow? What kinds of things are people doing in the snow?
9. As an extension to the experience, have children make a snow collage. Using blue construction paper as the background, create a snow scene. Tear pieces of white Magic Nuudle® construction paper. Brush lightly with water and stick to the blue construction paper. Using other colors, add details, such as trees, people, animals.

Table 3.21 Literacy Skills Nurtured in the Snow Experience

Visual Perception & Discrimination	Sequencing	Language Acquisition	Fine Motor	Gross Motor	Hand-Eye Coordination	Critical Thinking
●		●	●		●	

What Children Will Learn:

- **Hand-eye coordination, fine motor, and visual perception skills**—Playing with the snowflakes on the light table and comparing them to pictures of snowflakes in the books. Making patterns using different sizes of snowflakes on a light table.
- **Critical thinking skills**—Discussing the details of the snow painting; designing their own snow collage.

Art Experience 22: Recycled Rainbows

Language Art Benchmarks:

Listening and Speaking Standard 8 (Level Pre-K)

- Speaks clearly enough to be understood by unfamiliar adults and uses appropriate levels of volume, tone, and inflection
- Uses new vocabulary to describe feelings, thoughts, experiences, and observations
- Uses descriptive language (e.g., color words; size words, such as bigger, smaller; shape words)
- Asks questions to obtain information
- Answers simple questions
- Follows conversation rules (e.g., taking turns, making relevant comments; staying on topic) when talking with peers and adults
- Listens for a variety of purposes (e.g., to gain and share information, to perform a task, for enjoyment, to learn what happened in a story, to converse with an adult or peer)
- Understands messages in conversations (e.g. responds differently based on purpose of messages in conversation; attends and responds to conversations)

Suggested Vocabulary Words:

Rainbow, prism, recycled, words to describe the materials used, such as scrunchy, rough, etc.

Materials Needed:

Assorted recycled materials that are clean and not sharp (for example: buttons, cellophane paper, assorted fabric pieces, pipe cleaners, and drinking straws)

White butcher paper

Books on rainbows

Procedure:

1. Cover the table with white butcher paper.
2. Talk about rainbows with the children.
3. Read the book *A Rainbow of My Own* by Don Freeman.
4. Using the assorted recycled materials, have the children design a rainbow on the white paper.
5. Talk about the different kinds of materials used and their colors.

What Children Will Learn:

- **Hand-eye coordination, fine motor, and visual perception skills**—Selecting materials to use in their rainbows.
- **Language**—Discussing the characteristics of the materials with adults or peers.

Table 3.22 Literacy Skills Nurtured in the Recycled Rainbow Activity

Visual Perception & Discrimination	Sequencing	Language Acquisition	Fine Motor	Gross Motor	Hand-Eye Coordination	Critical Thinking
●		●	●		●	

Game 1: Color In the Masterpiece

Language Art Benchmarks:

Writing Standard 1 (Level Pre-K)

- Uses drawings to express thoughts, feelings, and ideas
- Uses forms of emergent writing (e.g., scribble writing, random symbols random letter-like marks) to represent ideas
- Uses writing tools and materials (e.g., pencils, crayons, chalk, markers, rubber stamps, computers, paper, cardboard, chalkboard)

Listening and Speaking Standard 8 (Level Pre-K)

- Uses new vocabulary to describe feelings, thoughts, experiences, and observations
- Uses descriptive language (e.g., color words; size words, such as bigger, smaller; shape words)

National Visual Arts Standards:

Understanding and Applying Media, Techniques, and Processes

- Knows the difference between materials and techniques
- Describes how different materials, techniques, and processes cause different responses
- Uses different media, techniques, and processes to communicate ideas, experiences, and stories
- Uses art materials and tools in a safe and responsible manner

Suggested Vocabulary Words:

Portrait, landscape, still life

Materials Needed:

Make copies of portions of artworks, such as a portrait showing only the face, but no body or clothing

Assorted markers or colored pencils

Procedure:

This game can be played using any work of art, but preferably portraits, provided that they can be reproduced by copying. Make a black-and-white photocopy of a portion of the artwork for each child. For example, if you choose a portrait, a copy of just the head can be provided for each child. Ask the child to guess if the person is male or female, what the person might be wearing, the color of hair, eyes, etc. Have the child add these details, using markers, colored pencils, or crayons, to complete the picture. After the children have completed their drawings, take the class to visit the gallery where the work is housed, or share the art reproduction of the portrait in your classroom. Have the children compare similarities and differences between their own drawings and the original. Start a class discussion about the work and the children's interpretations. Bear in mind that there are no right or wrong answers. Individual interpretations are most important here. Interpretation is an important skill in reading.

What Children Will Learn:

- **Critical thinking skills**—Interpreting the clues given with just a partial picture.
- **Visual discrimination, fine motor, and hand-eye coordination skills**—Drawing the rest of the picture.

All skills used during this game are key to future writing.

Table 3.23 Literacy Skills Nurtured in the Color in the Masterpiece Game

Visual Perception & Discrimination	Sequencing	Language Acquisition	Fine Motor	Gross Motor	Hand-Eye Coordination	Critical Thinking
●			●		●	●

Game 2: Words That Describe a Painting

Language Art Benchmarks:

Writing Standard 2 (level 1)

- Uses descriptive words to convey basic ideas

Reading Standard 5 (pre-K)

- Understands that illustrations and pictures convey meaning

Listening and Speaking Standard 8 (Level Pre-K)

- Uses new vocabulary to describe feelings, thoughts, experiences, and observations
- Uses descriptive language (e.g., color words; size words, such as bigger, smaller; shape words)
- Tells stories based on personal experience or make-believe
- Follows conversation rules (e.g., taking turns, making relevant comments; staying on topic) when talking with peers and adults

National Visual Arts Standards:

Understanding and Applying Media, Techniques, and Processes

- Knows the difference between materials and techniques
- Describes how different materials, techniques, and processes cause different responses
- Uses different media, techniques, and processes to communicate ideas, experiences, and stories
- Uses art materials and tools in a safe and responsible manner

Materials Needed:

A reproduction of an artwork

Vocabulary words written on slips of paper

Procedure:

This game can be played with children age 5 and older. Write a variety of descriptive words or adjectives on 3-inch by 5-inch note cards, with one word on each card. Select words that are developmentally appropriate and familiar to the children. Post an artwork for viewing. Give each child an adjective or noun card. As children view the artwork, ask them to match their adjective or noun to the painting, and then explain how their word can be used to describe it.

What Children Will Learn:

- **Language acquisition and critical thinking skills**—Explaining how a word describes a work of art.
- **Visual perception and discrimination skills**—Searching for clues in the artwork.

Table 3.24 Literacy Skills Nurtured in the Words that Describe a Painting Game

Visual Perception & Discrimination	Sequencing	Language Acquisition	Fine Motor	Gross Motor	Hand-Eye Coordination	Critical Thinking
●		●				●

Game 3: The Alphabet Game

Language Art Benchmarks:

Reading Standard 5 (Level Pre-K)

- Understands that illustrations and pictures convey meaning

Listening and Speaking Standard 8 (Level Pre-K)

- Uses new vocabulary to describe feelings, thoughts, experiences, and observations
- Uses descriptive language (e.g., color words; size words, such as bigger, smaller; shape words)
- Tells stories based on personal experience or make-believe
- Follows conversation rules (e.g., taking turns, making relevant comments; staying on topic) when talking with peers and adults

National Visual Arts Standards:

Using Knowledge of Structures and Functions

- Knows the differences among visual characteristics and purposes of art in order to convey ideas
- Describes how different expressive features and organizational principles cause different responses
- Uses visual structures and functions of art to communicate ideas

Choosing and Evaluating a Range of Subject Matter, Symbols, and Ideas

- Explores and understands prospective content for works of art
- Selects & uses subject matter, symbols, and ideas to communicate meaning
- Knows the visual arts have both a history and specific relationships to various cultures

Procedure:

After selecting an artwork as the focal point, ask children to sit in a circle in front of the work. Create your own game board and spinner from a cardboard circle with the alphabet letters written around the edge. Place an arrow spinner in the middle. The first child spins. When the spinner stops at a letter, ask the child to think of a word that begins with that letter to describe the artwork. Continue until all children have spun for a letter and chosen a word.

What Children Will Learn:

- **The alphabet.**
- **Critical thinking, language acquisition, and visual discrimination skills**—Scanning an artwork to come up with a word to describe or interpret the artwork.

Table 3.25 Literacy Skills Nurtured in the Alphabet Game

Visual Perception & Discrimination	Sequencing	Language Acquisition	Fine Motor	Gross Motor	Hand-Eye Coordination	Critical Thinking
●		●				●

Game 4: Storytelling

Language Art Benchmarks:

Listening and Speaking Standard 8 (Level Pre-K)

- Speaks clearly enough to be understood by unfamiliar adults and uses appropriate levels of volume, tone, and inflection
- Uses new vocabulary to describe feelings, thoughts, experiences, and observations
- Uses descriptive language (e.g., color words; size words, such as bigger, smaller; shape words)
- Asks questions to obtain information
- Answers simple questions
- Follows conversation rules (e.g., taking turns, making relevant comments; staying on topic) when talking with peers and adults
- Listens for a variety of purposes (e.g., to gain and share information, to perform a task, for enjoyment, to learn what happened in a story, to converse with an adult or peer)
- Understands messages in conversations (e.g., responds differently based on purpose of messages in conversation; attends and responds to conversations)
- Follows one- and two-step directions

Materials Needed:

An artwork displayed in the room at children's eye level

Procedure:

Ask children to focus on a painting in a museum or an art reproduction in your classroom. Tell them that they will play a game by telling a story about the painting. Begin the story by saying, "Once upon a time ...." Stop the story midstream and choose a child to continue the story. When that child stops, he or she chooses another child to continue. The process is completed when each child has had a turn to tell his or her part of the story about the artwork.

What Children Will Learn:

- **Vocabulary**—Listening to peers tell a story about the characters in an artwork.
- **Visual perception, critical thinking, and sequencing**—Scanning the artwork for story cues.

Table 3.26 Literacy Skills Nurtured in the Storytelling Game

Visual Perception & Discrimination	Sequencing	Language Acquisition	Fine Motor	Gross Motor	Hand-Eye Coordination	Critical Thinking
●	●	●				●

Game 5: Guess What's on My Glasses

Language Art Benchmarks:

Listening and Speaking Standard 8 (Level Pre-K)

- Speaks clearly enough to be understood by unfamiliar adults and uses appropriate levels of volume, tone, and inflection
- Uses new vocabulary to describe feelings, thoughts, experiences, and observations
- Uses descriptive language (e.g., color words; size words, such as bigger, smaller; shape words)
- Asks questions to obtain information
- Answers simple questions
- Follows conversation rules (e.g., taking turns, making relevant comments; staying on topic) when talking with peers and adults
- Listens for a variety of purposes (e.g., to gain and share information, to perform a task, for enjoyment, to learn what happened in a story, to converse with an adult or peer)
- Understands messages in conversations (e.g., responds differently based on purpose of messages in conversation; attends and responds to conversations)
- Follows one- and two-step directions

Suggested Vocabulary Words:

The artwork used for this game will dictate which vocabulary words are used

Materials Needed:

Cardboard eyeglasses

Postcard-size art reproduction

Various art reproductions displayed around the room

Procedure:

Glue a small reproduction of a painting to the top of a pair of cardboard glasses without lenses. Place the glasses on a child without letting the child see the art reproduction. Lead the child into the gallery or classroom area where, among numerous other paintings, there is a match for the painting on the glasses. The teacher or children then describe to the child wearing the glasses what the painting looks like. After the verbal description, ask the child, "Can you find the painting? Show me where." The game continues with verbal cues from the teacher and children until the child correctly identifies the painting. This game can be played in groups of three or four with one child from each group wearing the glasses. The members of the group offer verbal cues until the correct choice is made.

What Children Will Learn:

- **Social experience and language skills**—Providing verbal clues to a peer.
- **Visual discrimination and critical thinking skills**—Carefully examining the painting for clues.

Table 3.27 Literacy Skills Nurtured in Guess What is on My Glasses Game

Visual Perception & Discrimination	Sequencing	Language Acquisition	Fine Motor	Gross Motor	Hand-Eye Coordination	Critical Thinking
●		●				●

Game 6: Art Twister

Language Art Benchmarks:

Listening and Speaking Standard 8 (Level Pre-K)

- Understands messages in conversations (e.g., responds differently based on purpose of messages in conversation; attends and responds to conversations)
- Follows one- and two-step directions

Suggested Vocabulary Words:

Over, under, around, left, right

Materials Needed:

8 ½-inch by 11-inch plastic sheet protectors (16 total)

8 ½ -inch by 11-inch color reproductions (16 total)

5-inch by 7-inch art reproductions (same images as the 8 ½-inch by 11-inch reproductions)

Clear wide tape

Masking tape

Procedure:

Place one color art reproduction in each plastic sleeve. Place plastic sleeves side by side, making a grid pattern of four columns and four rows. Tape sections together with clear wide plastic tape—this is your "art twister mat." To play the game, place the 5-inch by 7-inch art images on a body part of each child, securing them in place with masking tape. For example, use knees, elbows, head, etc. Have children line up in front of the art twister mat, which is placed on the floor. Each child finds the image on the mat that is taped to his or her body. He or she places that body part on the image. Tell children that whoever falls down is out of the game. The game is played until there is one player remaining.

What Children Will Learn:

- **Visual discrimination skills**—Matching their image with the one on the art twister mat.

Table 3.28 Literacy Skills Nurtured in Art Twister

Visual Perception & Discrimination	Sequencing	Language Acquisition	Fine Motor	Gross Motor	Hand-Eye Coordination	Critical Thinking
●						

Detailed Symbols as Meaning Makers

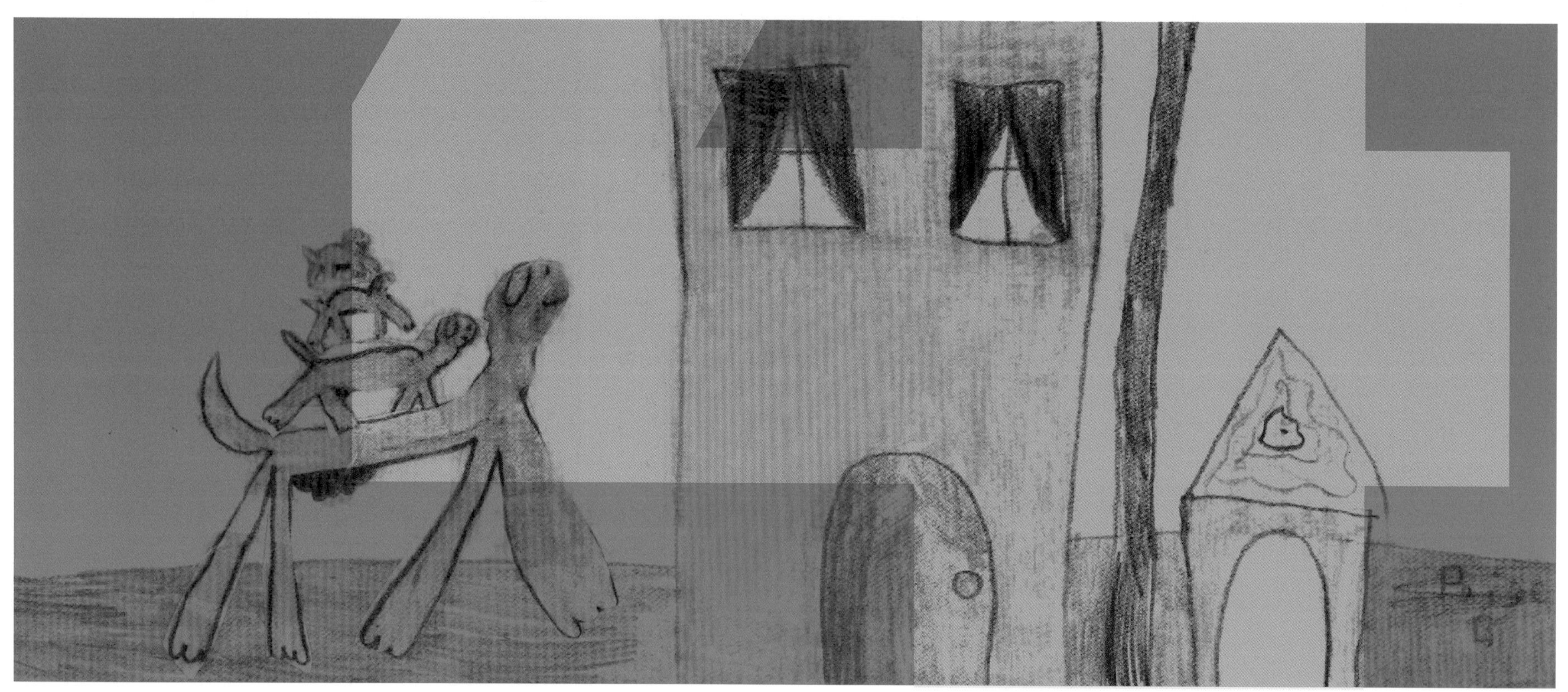

Picture 4.1 Ground Line

Picture 4.2: Picture With Clothed Figures

Characteristics of Children Who Draw as Meaning Makers

This phase ushers in dramatic changes in the child's graphic and three-dimensional creations. By this time, the child has developed an extensive semiotic vocabulary, "which begins to successfully carry meaning which can be shared socially and appear to be independent of verbal narrative or supporting gestural cues" (Kindler, 1997, p. 31). Children's skills in using various materials have improved, so their drawings of symbols for animate and inanimate objects look more like they intended.

Children in this phase typically draw symbols for objects in a bold and direct flat representation. If the child intends to draw in a more realistic fashion, he or she sometimes still struggles with spatial representation; therefore, perspective and dimension are still lacking in their drawings. Children's drawings of the human form are perfected by the addition of more details in the anatomy. Clothing is given more detail as children begin to add designs to shirts, dresses, and other clothing articles. The child also becomes more organized in the use of space by placing objects and people on the ground line. Overall, "the improved control over a drawing tool results in images that conform more closely to the common societal expectations of what a drawing should be like" (Kindler, 1997, p. 31). Because children at this phase are drawing with greater detail, they may create "X-ray drawings," depending on the culture, where both the inside and outside of an object are portrayed. For example, some drawings show the legs through the trousers. Drawings can also begin to reveal multiple perspectives, almost in a Picasso-like fashion. For example, a train is drawn displaying the side view, but the tracks are drawn from an aerial perspective.

This phase ushers in dramatic changes in the child's graphic and three-dimensional creations.

Picture 4.3: X-ray Picture

The use of color goes through a striking change during this phase. Once again, if the child intends to portray realism, he or she is now careful to use the "correct" color of the object in real life. Therefore, trees and grass are green, the sky and water are blue.

Because of their cognitive advances, children are able to write and tell more elaborate stories based on their drawings. Images from popular culture become part of the repertoire of children's graphic vocabulary. "They are part of children's everyday world … they are well entrenched in children's memories. Children often use names of superheroes to gain acceptance within a group" (Kolbe, 2005, p. 43).

When working with three-dimensional materials, such as clay, "children who have had ample experiences with clay and have been encouraged 'to see,' are able to use clay in increasingly complex ways" (Kolbe, 1997, p. 8).

Literacy Experiences During This Phase

During this phase, one can see the same type of development occur with letter and number symbols as was evidenced in the previous chapter when children exhibited interest in adding linear patterns that started to resemble letters and numbers. These children typically do not start writing in a coherent and clear manner, but rather interject individual letters and numbers into their artwork to represent a concept, thought, or big idea (Clay, 1995; Dyson, 1993). As children continue to explore these letters and numbers in this phase, they try to replicate adult-like writing behavior. This is evident when children incorporate traditional literacy symbols, like letters or numbers, into their artwork.

The more language and literacy experiences that children experience in their daily interactions, the more they show evidence of language use in their artwork. Children begin to use emergent writing, which means that they "understand that writing is a form of communication and their marks on paper convey a message. Emergent forms of writing include drawing, scribbling from left to right, creating letter like forms, or creating random strings of letters, all used—sometimes even simultaneously—in the child's attempt to communicate an idea through print" (Mayer, 2007, p. 35).

We see a pattern of change as children subtly replace images with the written word. During this time, providing kinesthetic art experiences, such as forming letters with flexible wires, can reinforce literacy success.

Art Experiences for This Phase

We provide visual art experiences that parents and teachers can implement to help promote early literacy development with young children in the primary grades.

Aesthetic Preferences of Children During This Phase

During this phase, many children go through striking changes in their aesthetic preferences. They no longer favor abstract artwork, but tend to favor more realistic renderings, especially ones that appear to have been executed with a lot of skill and effort. Color must appear realistic and used almost in a photograph-like way. Subject matter that children earlier found frightening or even gory is now accepted (Gardner & Winner, 1976; Hardiman & Zernich, 1977, 1982; Machotka, 1966; Parsons, 1987; Taunton, 1980; Kerlavage, 1995).

While any artworks can be used for the games at the end of the chapter, more realistic may be most suitable. However, bear in mind that realism is not always preferred by children
in some cultures. Therefore, having the children select the works to be used might be the best practice.

Art Experience 1: Wire Sculpture

Language Art Benchmarks:

Listening and Speaking Standard 8 (Level 1)

- Gives and responds to oral directions

Viewing Standard 9 (Level 1)

- Understands the main idea or message in visual media (e.g., pictures, cartoons, weather reports on television, newspaper photographs, visual narratives)

National Visual Arts Standards:

Understanding and Applying Media, Techniques, and Processes

- Knows the difference between materials and techniques
- Describes how different materials, techniques, and processes cause different responses
- Uses art materials and tools in a safe and responsible manner

Using Knowledge of Structures and Functions

- Knows the differences among visual characteristics and purposes of art in order to convey ideas

Choosing and Evaluating a Range of Subject Matter, Symbols, and Ideas

- Selects and uses subject matter, symbols, and ideas to communicate meaning

Suggested Vocabulary Words:

Sculpture, form, shape

Materials Needed:

Clothesline wire

Assorted beads, pipe cleaners, buttons

Styrofoam base

Large window or mirror

Procedure:

1. Cut clothesline or electrical wire into various lengths.
2. Have children string a variety of beads onto the wire in random patterns.
3. Twist and form the wire into any shape.
4. Invite children to attach other wire forms to add to the group sculpture piece.
5. Change the sculpture piece at any time by adding more beads and moving the wires. Experiment by adding other items to the clothesline wire, such as pipe cleaners, feathers, assorted papers, large buttons, etc.
6. Attach the wire sculpture to a Styrofoam base so it stands securely.

What Children Will Learn:

- **Visual perception and discrimination**—Selecting different colors and shapes of beads used to create patterns.
- **Sequencing**—Creating patterns to form a sequence. Sequencing is an important component of literacy in a variety of ways: sequences of letters create words, sequences of words create sentences, and a sequence of events creates a story.
- **Hand-eye coordination and fine motor skills**—Selecting materials that are strung through the wire. These skills contribute to children's ability to properly grasp a writing instrument while they write.
- **Language acquisition**—Learning new words in relation to sculpture.

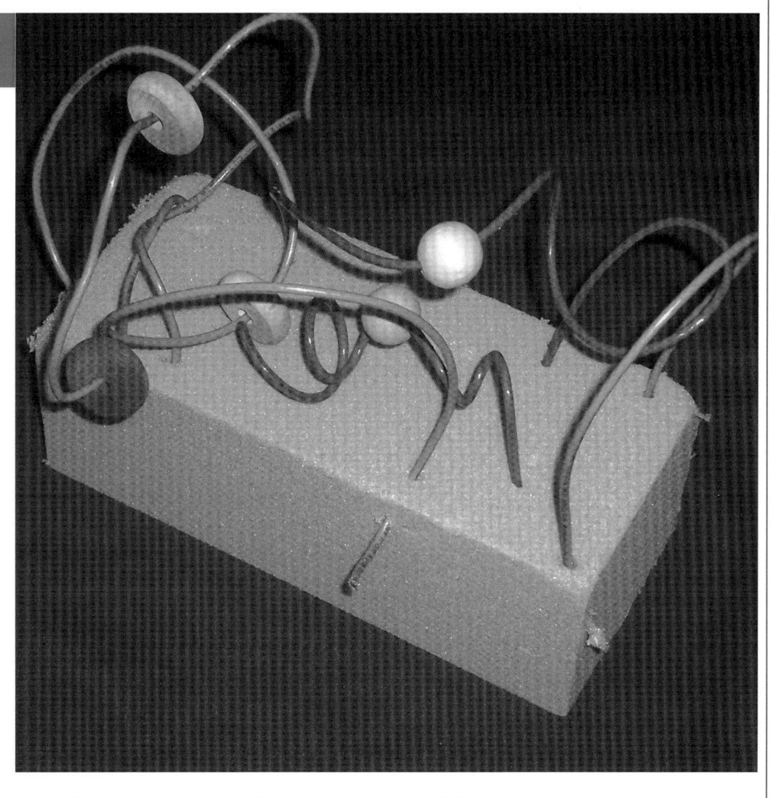

Table 4.1 Literacy Skills Nurtured in the Wire Sculpture Experience

Visual Perception & Discrimination	Sequencing	Language Acquisition	Fine Motor	Gross Motor	Hand-Eye Coordination	Critical Thinking
●	●	●	●		●	

Art Experience 2: Shadow Puppets

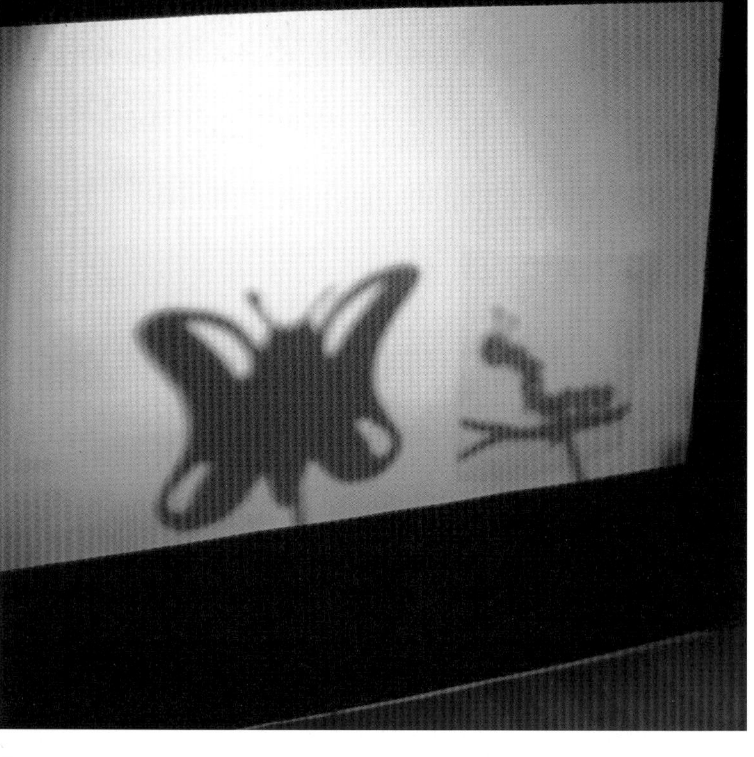

Language Art Benchmarks:

Listening and Speaking Standard 8 (Level 1)

- Makes contributions in class and group discussions (e.g., reports on ideas and personal knowledge about a topic, initiates conversations, connects ideas and experiences with those of others)
- Asks and responds to questions (e.g., about the meaning of a story, about the meaning of words or ideas)
- Follows rules of conversation and group discussion (e.g., takes turns, raises hand to speak, stays on topic, focuses attention on speaker)
- Uses different voice level, phrasing, and intonation for different situations (e.g., small group settings, informal discussions, reports to the class)
- Uses level-appropriate vocabulary in speech (e.g., number words; words that describe people, places, things, events, location, actions; synonyms, antonyms; homonyms, word analogies, common figures of speech)
- Recites and responds to familiar stories, poems, and rhymes with patterns (e.g., relates information to own life; describes character, setting, plot)

Viewing Standard 9

- Knows how different elements help to establish plot, setting, and character in visual narratives (e.g., action, dialogue, music, clothing, facial expressions)
- Knows different features (e.g., facial expressions, body language, gesture, clothing, actions, relationships, dialogue) that affect a viewer's perceptions of characters in visual media (e.g., qualities that identify a "hero" or a "villain")

Suggested Vocabulary Words:

Puppet, shadow, transparent

National Visual Arts Standards:

Understanding and Applying Media, Techniques, and Processes

- Knows the difference between materials and techniques
- Uses art materials and tools in a safe and responsible manner

Knowledge of Structures and Functions

- Knows the differences among visual characteristics and purposes of art in order to convey ideas

Choosing and Evaluating a Range of Subject Matter, Symbols, and Ideas

- Selects and uses subject matter, symbols, and ideas to communicate meaning

Reflecting Upon and Assessing the Characteristics and Merits of Their Work and the Work of Others

- Understands there are different responses to specific artworks
-

Materials Needed:

Crayola Gel FX markers
Clear acetate sheets
Scissors
Clear drinking straws
Clear tape
Puppet theater
Vellum paper
Flashlight or overhead projector

Procedure:

1. On a sheet of clear acetate, draw any character (animal, person, make-believe creature) of your choice using Gel FX markers.
2. Using scissors, cut out the character.
3. Tape a drinking straw to the bottom of the puppet.
4. Place the new puppet behind a vellum screen with a light source shining from behind. Vellum can easily be attached with tape to any puppet theater stage. Use white tissue paper as a substitute for vellum.
5. Add background scenery by drawing on larger clear acetate sheets.

Table 4.2 Literacy Skills Nurtured in the Shadow Puppet Experience

Visual Perception & Discrimination	Sequencing	Language Acquisition	Fine Motor	Gross Motor	Hand-Eye Coordination	Critical Thinking
●	●	●	●		●	●

What Children Will Learn:

- **Visual perception and discrimination, fine motor and hand-eye coordination**—Selecting the materials and creating the puppets.
- **Sequencing and language acquisition**—Engaging in the storytelling process with the characters they created.
- **Critical thinking**—Creating the puppets and telling the puppets' stories.
- **Construct a story in a logical sequence**—Putting their thoughts into words in an organized fashion and then organizing words into a story.

Art Experience 3: Accordion-Fold Puppets

Language Art Benchmarks:

Listening and Speaking Standard 8 (Level 1)

- Makes contributions in class and group discussions (e.g., reports on ideas and personal knowledge about a topic, initiates conversations, connects ideas and experiences with those of others)
- Asks and responds to questions (e.g., about the meaning of a story, about the meaning of words or ideas)
- Follows rules of conversation and group discussion (e.g., takes turns, raises hand to speak, stays on topic, focuses attention on speaker)
- Uses different voice level, phrasing, and intonation for different situations (e.g., small group settings, informal discussions, reports to the class)
- Uses level-appropriate vocabulary in speech (e.g., number words; words that describe people, places, things, events, location, actions; synonyms, antonyms; homonyms, word analogies, common figures of speech)
- Recites and responds to familiar stories, poems, and rhymes with patterns (e.g., relates information to own life; describes character, setting, plot)

Viewing Standard 9 (Level 1)

- Knows how different elements help to establish plot, setting, and character in visual narratives (e.g., action, dialogue, music, clothing, facial expressions)
- Knows different features (e.g., facial expressions, body language, gesture, clothing, actions, relationships, dialogue) that affect a viewer's perceptions of characters in visual media (e.g., qualities that identify a "hero" or a "villain")

Suggested Vocabulary Words:

Accordion fold, vertical

Materials Needed:

8-inch by 11-inch construction paper in assorted colors

Variety of scrap papers

Scissors

Glue

Procedure:

1. Fold a sheet of construction paper into thirds lengthwise.
2. Fold in half with the top and bottom meeting.
3. Fold again in half with the opening flap on the outside.
4. Slip your thumb and fingers into the slots to make the puppet talk.
5. Create features by gluing on scrap papers to make any character desired.
6. Children can tell a story using their created puppets as the characters in their own puppet show.

What Children Will Learn:

- **Visual perception and discrimination, fine motor, and hand-eye coordination**—Selecting materials and creating puppets.
- **Sequencing and language acquisition**—Engaging in the storytelling process with the characters they created.
- **Critical thinking**—Creating the puppets and telling puppets' stories in a play.

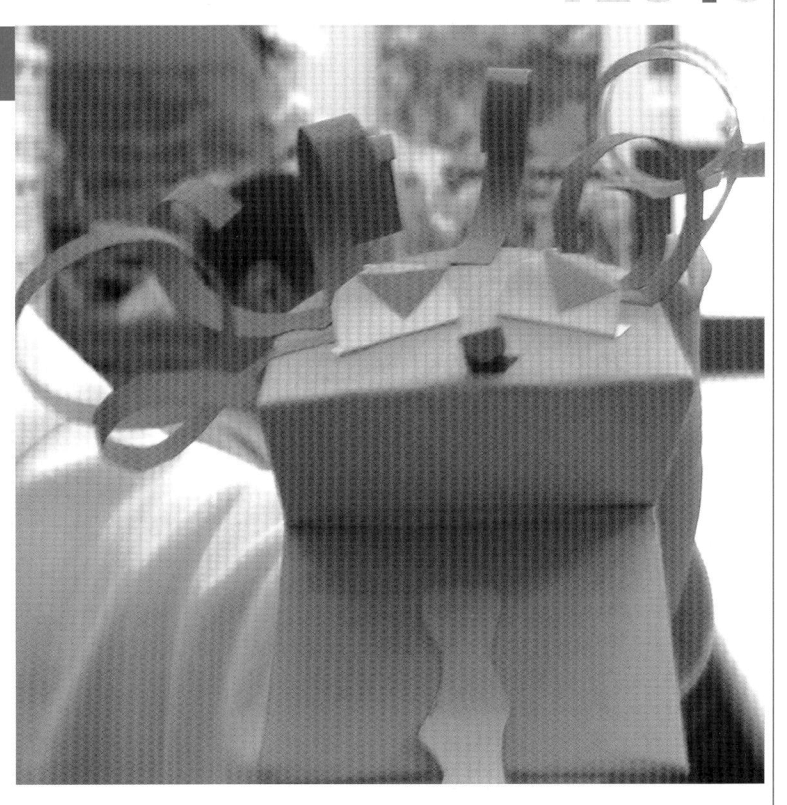

Table 4.3 Literacy Skills Nurtured in the Accordion Puppets Experience

Visual Perception & Discrimination	Sequencing	Language Acquisition	Fine Motor	Gross Motor	Hand-Eye Coordination	Critical Thinking
●	●	●	●		●	●

National Visual Arts Standards:

Understanding and Applying Media, Techniques, and Processes

- Knows the difference between materials & techniques
- Uses art materials and tools in a safe and responsible manner

Using Knowledge of Structures and Functions

- Knows the differences among visual characteristics and purposes of art in order to convey ideas

Choosing and Evaluating a Range of Subject Matter, Symbols, and Ideas

- Selects and uses subject matter, symbols, and ideas to communicate meaning

Reflecting Upon and Assessing the Characteristics and Merits of Their Work and the Work of Others

- Understands there are different responses to specific artworks

Art Experience 4: Whimsical Paper Sculptures

Language Art Benchmarks:

Listening and Speaking Standard 8 (Level 1)

- Makes contributions in class and group discussions (e.g., reports on ideas and personal knowledge about a topic, initiates conversations, connects ideas and experiences with those of others)
- Asks and responds to questions (e.g., about the meaning of a story, about the meaning of words or ideas)
- Follows rules of conversation and group discussion (e.g., takes turns, raises hand to speak, stays on topic, focuses attention on speaker)
- Uses level-appropriate vocabulary in speech (e.g., number words; words that describe people, places, things, events, location, actions; synonyms, antonyms; homonyms, word analogies, common figures of speech)

National Visual Arts Standards:

Understanding and Applying Media, Techniques, and Processes

- Knows the difference between materials and techniques
- Uses art materials and tools in a safe and responsible manner

Using Knowledge of Structures and Functions

- Knows the differences among visual characteristics and purposes of art in order to convey ideas

Choosing and Evaluating a Range of Subject Matter, Symbols, and Ideas

- Selects and uses subject matter, symbols, and ideas to communicate meaning

Reflecting Upon and Assessing the Characteristics and Merits of Their Work and the Work of Others

- Understands there are different responses to specific artworks

Materials Needed:

Card-stock paper in a variety of colors

Scissors (optional)

Book: *Don't Worry, Be Happy* by Bobby McFerrin

Song: "Don't Worry, Be Happy" by Bobby McFerrin

Visuals of Alexander Calder's sculptures (found in Bobby McFerrin book, or downloading images from the Internet)

Procedure:

1. Read the book *Don't Worry, Be Happy* by Bobby McFerrin. Talk about the various sculpture pieces as portrayed in the book. Have children identify the many different geometric shapes of the sculptures.
2. Cut or tear card stock into geometric or free-form shapes no larger than 5 inches.
3. To join pieces, cut a slit halfway up on each piece of cardstock.
4. Join pieces by sliding one slit into another.
5. Add pieces to make a free-standing 3-D sculpture.
6. While children are working, play the song "Don't Worry, Be Happy" by Bobby McFerrin.
7. Invite children to write a story about their sculpture piece and answer questions such as: Where will the sculpture be best placed in the community?

Suggested Vocabulary Words:

Sculpture, form, space, attach, join

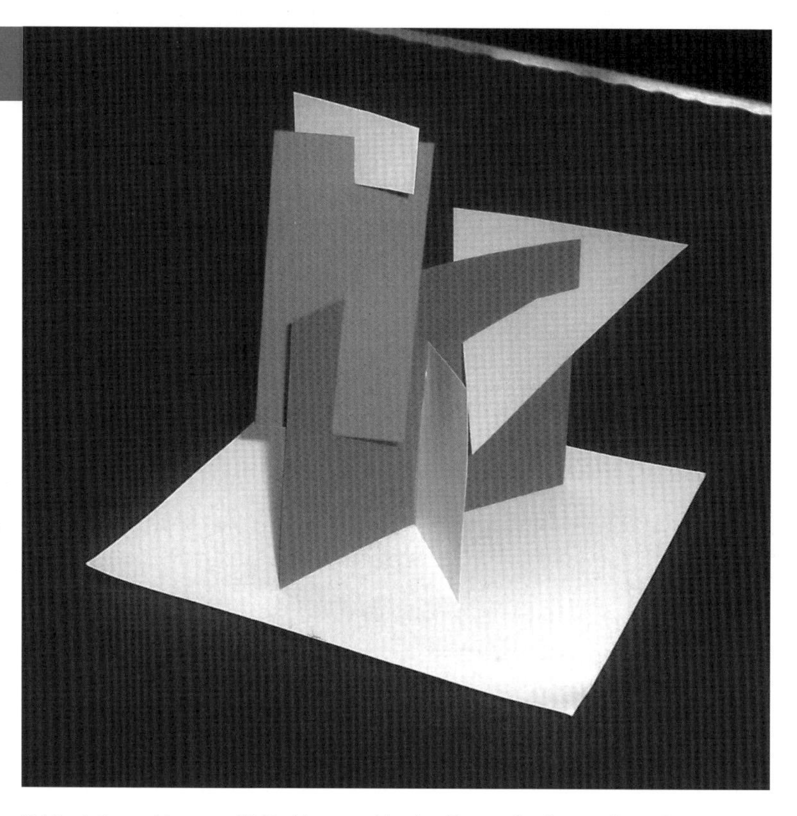

Table 4.4 Literacy Skills Nurtured in the Paper Sculpture Experience

Visual Perception & Discrimination	Sequencing	Language Acquisition	Fine Motor	Gross Motor	Hand-Eye Coordination	Critical Thinking
●			●		●	●

What Children Will Learn:

- **Visual perception**—Studying the Calder sculptures as a reference in helping them create their own works.
- **Fine motor and hand-eye coordination skills**—Participating in the sculpture construction process (tearing and cutting of paper, joining of paper to form sculptures).
- **Critical thinking**—Exploring and figuring out how to connect the pieces and materials to create a three-dimensional form.

Art Experience 5: Color Collage

Language Art Benchmarks:

Writing Standard 1 (Level 1)

- Uses writing and other methods (e.g., using letters or phonetically spelled words, telling, dictating, making lists) to describe familiar persons, places, objects, or experiences
- Writes for different purposes (e.g., to entertain, inform, learn, communicate ideas)

Writing Standard 2 (Level 1)

- Uses descriptive words to convey basic ideas

Writing Standard 3 (Level 1)

- Uses adjectives in written compositions (e.g., uses descriptive words)

Listening and Speaking Standard 8 (Level 1)

- Asks and responds to questions (e.g., about the meaning of a story, about the meaning of words or ideas)
- Follows rules of conversation and group discussion (e.g., takes turns, raises hand to speak, stays on topic, focuses attention on speaker)
- Uses level-appropriate vocabulary in speech (e.g., number words; words that describe people, places, things, events, location, actions; synonyms, antonyms; homonyms, word analogies, common figures of speech)

Suggested Vocabulary Words:

Collage, hue, variation, overlap

Materials Needed:

8 ½-inch by 11-inch paper
Assorted magazines
Glue stick
Scissors
Assorted markers

National Visual Arts Standards:

Understanding and Applying Media, Techniques, and Processes

- Knows the difference between materials and techniques
- Describes how different materials, techniques, and processes cause different responses
- Uses art materials and tools in a safe and responsible manner

Using Knowledge of Structures and Functions

- Knows the differences among visual characteristics and purposes of art in order to convey ideas

Choosing and Evaluating a Range of Subject Matter, Symbols, and Ideas

- Selects and uses subject matter, symbols, and ideas to communicate meaning

Reflecting Upon and Assessing the Characteristics and Merits of Their Work and the Work of Others

- Understands there are different responses to specific artworks

Procedure:

1. Read *My Many Colored Days* by Dr. Seuss.
2. Talk about colors and how they make us feel.
3. Have children choose their favorite color.
4. Look for swatches of that color in magazines and tear or cut them out.
5. Glue these color swatches onto a piece of 8 ½-inch by 11-inch paper, leaving a 1-inch border.
6. Using a marker of the same color as the collage, write how the color makes you feel. Write in the border area of the collage, perhaps encircling the collage.

Table 4.5 Literacy Skills Nurtured in the Color Collage Experience

Visual Perception & Discrimination	Sequencing	Language Acquisition	Fine Motor	Gross Motor	Hand-Eye Coordination	Critical Thinking
●		●	●		●	●

What Children Will Learn:

- **Visual discrimination skills**—Selecting examples of their colors.
- **Writing skills**—Writing about their feelings about their color choice, which uses fine motor skills and hand-eye coordination.
- **Critical thinking skills**—Describing the way the colors of the collage make them feel.

Art Experience 6: Descriptive Letter Art

Language Art Benchmarks:

Writing Standard 1 (Level 1)

- Writes for different purposes (e.g., to entertain, inform, learn, communicate ideas)

Writing Standard 2 (Level 1)

- Uses descriptive words to convey basic ideas

Writing Standard 3 (Level 1)

- Uses adjectives in written compositions (e.g., uses descriptive words)

Listening and Speaking Standard 8(Level 1)

- Asks and responds to questions (e.g., about the meaning of a story, about the meaning of words or ideas)
- Follows rules of conversation and group discussion (e.g., takes turns, raises hand to speak, stays on topic, focuses attention on speaker)
- Uses level-appropriate vocabulary in speech (e.g., number words; words that describe people, places, things, events, location, actions; synonyms, antonyms; homonyms, word analogies, common figures of speech)

Suggested Vocabulary Words:

Encourage children to use their own acquired vocabulary for this project.

Materials Needed:

8 ½-inch by 11-inch paper

Letter suggestions typed on each paper—for example, an angry "A"; a bubbly "B," etc.

Crayons or markers

Procedure:

1. Look at the popular media for examples of letters that help to portray the meaning of a word. Discuss this with the children.
2. Think of ways to describe each letter of the alphabet and type them on the bottom of each sheet of paper. Examples are: angry "A"; bubbly "B"; crying "C"; dancing "D." Have children help with this process.
3. Give each child one of these papers and have the child draw the letter as described using crayons or markers.

National Visual Arts Standards:

Understanding and Applying Media, Techniques, and Processes

- Describes how different materials, techniques, and processes cause different responses

Using Knowledge of Structures and Functions

- Knows the differences among visual characteristics and purposes of art in order to convey ideas

Choosing and Evaluating a Range of Subject Matter, Symbols, and Ideas

- Selects and uses subject matter, symbols, and ideas to communicate meaning

Reflecting Upon and Assessing the Characteristics and Merits of Their Work and the Work of Others

- Understands there are different responses to specific artworks

Table 4.6 Literacy Skills Nurtured in Descriptive Letter Art

Visual Perception & Discrimination	Sequencing	Language Acquisition	Fine Motor	Gross Motor	Hand-Eye Coordination	Critical Thinking
●		●	●		●	●

What Children Will Learn:

- **Visual discrimination and perception skills**—Drawing their letter forms.
- **Language**—Using drawing to interpret the word that describes their letter.
- **Fine motor skills and hand-eye coordination**—Engaging in the drawing experience.
- **Critical thinking skills**—Describing, in a visual way, what the letter is demonstrating.

Art Experience 7: Penny-Roll Puppets

Language Art Benchmarks:

Listening and Speaking Standard 8 (Level 1)

- Makes contributions in class and group discussions (e.g., reports on ideas and personal knowledge about a topic, initiates conversations, connects ideas and experiences with those of others)
- Asks and responds to questions (e.g., about the meaning of a story, about the meaning of words or ideas)
- Follows rules of conversation and group discussion (e.g., takes turns, raises hand to speak, stays on topic, focuses attention on speaker)
- Uses different voice level, phrasing, and intonation for different situations (e.g., small group settings, informal discussions, reports to the class)
- Uses level-appropriate vocabulary in speech (e.g., number words; words that describe people, places, things, events, location, actions; synonyms, antonyms; homonyms, word analogies, common figures of speech)
- Recites and responds to familiar stories, poems, and rhymes with patterns (e.g., relates information to own life; describes character, setting, plot)

Viewing Standard 9 (Level 1)

- Knows how different elements help to establish plot, setting, and character in visual narratives (e.g., action, dialogue, music, clothing, facial expressions)
- Knows different features (e.g., facial expressions, body language, gesture, clothing, actions, relationships, dialogue) that affect a viewer's perceptions of characters in visual media (e.g., qualities that identify a "hero" or a "villain".

Suggested Vocabulary Words:

Penny roll, attach, finger puppet, assemble

Materials Needed:

Penny rolls
Scissors
Glue
Assorted colored scraps of paper

Procedure:

1. Have children think about a puppet character they would like to create.
2. Ask them to select colored papers and assorted scrap materials to create the character.
3. Use the penny roll as the body of the puppet. Cut body parts and clothing from the scrap paper and assorted materials and glue to the appropriate place on the penny roll.
4. Have children place their created penny-roll character on their finger and make the character come to life through drama.
5. Encourage them to write a puppet play and perform it with their puppet. This can be done individually or in groups.

What Children Will Learn:

- **Visual discrimination and perception skills**—Selecting colors of paper and creating their puppet character.
- **Language**—Make their puppet character come to life through drama.
- **Fine motor skills and hand-eye coordination**—Creating the puppet through cutting and gluing.
- **Critical thinking skills**—Deciding how to create their character and making that character come to life through dramatic play as a story is told.

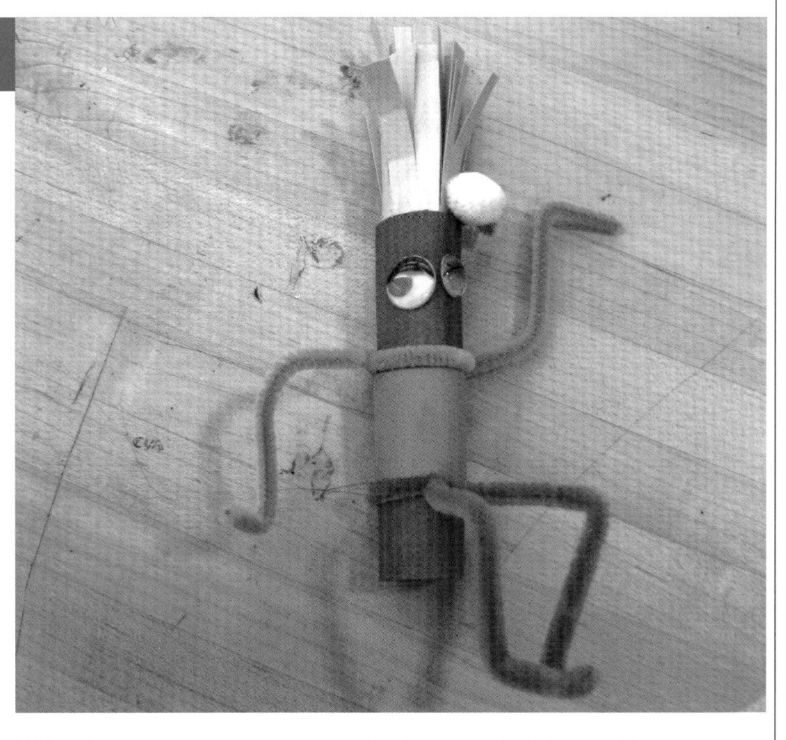

Table 4.7 Literacy Skills Nurtured in the Penny-Roll Puppet Experience

Visual Perception & Discrimination	Sequencing	Language Acquisition	Fine Motor	Gross Motor	Hand-Eye Coordination	Critical Thinking
●		●	●		●	●

National Visual Arts Standards:

Understanding and Applying Media, Techniques, and Processes

- Knows the difference between materials and techniques
- Uses art materials and tools in a safe and responsible manner

Using Knowledge of Structures and Functions

- Knows the differences among visual characteristics and purposes of art in order to convey ideas

Choosing and Evaluating a Range of Subject Matter, Symbols, and Ideas

- Selects and uses subject matter, symbols, and ideas to communicate meaning

Reflecting Upon and Assessing the Characteristics and Merits of Their Work and the Work of Others

- Understands there are different responses to specific artworks

Art Experience 8: Foam Letter Art

Language Art Benchmarks:

Viewing Standard 9 (Level 1)

- Knows how different elements help to establish plot, setting, and character in visual narratives (e.g., action, dialogue, music, clothing, facial expressions)
- Knows different features (e.g., facial expressions, body language, gesture, clothing, actions, relationships, dialogue) that affect a viewer's perceptions of characters in visual media (e.g., qualities that identify a "hero" or a "villain")

National Visual Arts Standards:

Understanding and Applying Media, Techniques, and Processes

- Knows the difference between materials and techniques
- Uses art materials and tools in a safe and responsible manner

Using Knowledge of Structures and Functions

- Knows the differences among visual characteristics and purposes of art in order to convey ideas

Choosing and Evaluating a Range of Subject Matter, Symbols, and Ideas

- Selects and uses subject matter, symbols, and ideas to communicate meaning

Reflecting Upon and Assessing the Characteristics and Merits of Their Work and the Work of Others

- Understands there are different responses to specific artworks

Suggested Vocabulary Words:

Encourage children to use their own acquired vocabulary for this project.

Materials Needed:

2-inch self-adhesive felt letters

Poster board cut into approximately 6-inch pieces

Assorted markers

Procedure:

1. Adhere one felt adhesive letter to each piece of poster board that has been cut to approximately a 6-inch square.
2. Each letter can be placed randomly on each cardboard piece.
3. Randomly distribute poster board to children.
4. Children can turn the poster board in any direction.
5. The letter will be used as a guide to draw an object, person, or animal that begins with that letter.
6. The letter must be a part of the drawing.
7. Share the book *Alphabet Under Construction* by Denise Fleming.

What Children Will Learn:

- **Critical thinking, visual perception, fine motor skills and hand-eye coordination**—Drawing a picture that incorporates the letter they were given.
- **Language acquisition**—Children have to come up with a word that begins with the letter.

Table 4.8 Literacy Skills Nurtured in the Foam Letter Experience

Visual Perception & Discrimination	Sequencing	Language Acquisition	Fine Motor	Gross Motor	Hand-Eye Coordination	Critical Thinking
●		●	●		●	●

Art Experience 9: Gargoyles

Language Art Benchmarks:

Viewing Standard 9 (Level 1)

- Knows how different elements help to establish plot, setting, and character in visual narratives (e.g., action, dialogue, music, clothing, facial expressions)
- Knows different features (e.g., facial expressions, body language, gesture, clothing, actions, relationships, dialogue) that affect a viewer's perceptions of characters in visual media (e.g., qualities that identify a "hero" or a "villain")

National Visual Arts Standards:

Understanding and Applying Media, Techniques, and Processes

- Knows the difference between materials and techniques
- Uses art materials and tools in a safe and responsible manner

Using Knowledge of Structures and Functions

- Knows the differences among visual characteristics and purposes of art in order to convey ideas

Choosing and Evaluating a Range of Subject Matter, Symbols, and Ideas

- Selects and uses subject matter, symbols, and ideas to communicate meaning

Reflecting Upon and Assessing the Characteristics and Merits of Their Work and the Work of Others

- Understands there are different responses to specific artworks

Suggested Vocabulary Words:

Gargoyle, cathedral, rain spout, sculpture

Materials Needed:

Neon-colored Model Magic (made by Crayola)

Visuals of gargoyles

Procedure:

1. Provide a historical background about gargoyles. In medieval times, artists created gargoyles to perch on top of many cathedrals. These grotesque animal-like creatures served two purposes: to ward off evil spirits and to serve as a rain spout. Many gargoyles still serve as sentries for European cathedrals today.
2. Show different examples of gargoyles and have the children guess what animals are represented.
3. Write the names of different animals on a strip of paper, one animal per strip.
4. Place these in a box and have the children choose two strips each. This will provide them with unlikely animal combinations that will inspire the making of a gargoyle.
5. Provide each child with several neon colors of Model Magic. Neon colors jazz up this experience and spur creative responses. If desired, you can use neutral colors of Model Magic as well.
6. Ask children to construct their gargoyle by incorporating the two animals chosen. Let dry overnight.
7. Ask children to come up with a name for their gargoyle and write a short story about the gargoyle. Have children share their stories with the class.
8. As an extension, invite children to design a building where their gargoyle can be perched. These buildings can be constructed out of any material desired, such cardboard boxes.

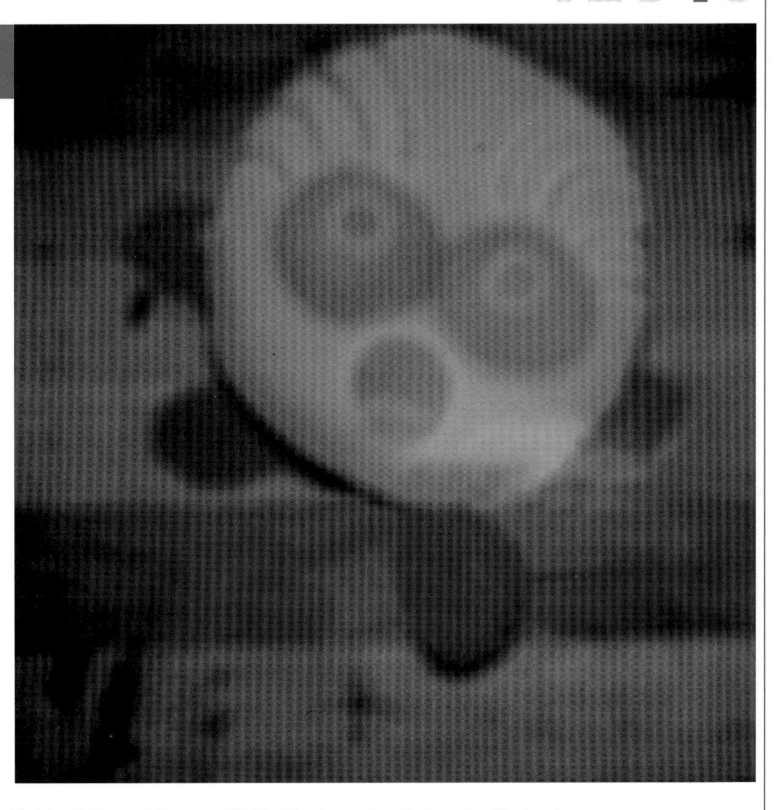

Table 4.9 Literacy Skills Nurtured in Gargoyle Project

Visual Perception & Discrimination	Problem Solving	Language Acquisition	Fine Motor	Gross Motor	Hand-Eye Coordination	Critical Thinking
●	●		●			

What Children Will Learn:

- **Critical thinking skills and problem solving**—Constructing their gargoyle and writing a story.
- **Visual perception skills**—Viewing different gargoyles and noticing the differences between them.
- **Fine motor skills**—Creating the gargoyle.

Art Experience 10: Drawing Crazy Creatures

Language Art Benchmarks:

Viewing Standard 9 (Level 1)

- Knows how different elements help to establish plot, setting, and character in visual narratives (e.g., action, dialogue, music, clothing, facial expressions)
- Knows different features (e.g., facial expressions, body language, gesture, clothing, actions, relationships, dialogue) that affect a viewer's perceptions of characters in visual media (e.g., qualities that identify a "hero" or a "villain")

National Visual Arts Standards:

Understanding and Applying Media, Techniques, and Processes

- Knows the difference between materials and techniques
- Uses art materials and tools in a safe and responsible manner

Using Knowledge of Structures and Functions

- Knows the differences among visual characteristics and purposes of art in order to convey ideas

Choosing and Evaluating a Range of Subject Matter, Symbols, and Ideas

- Selects and uses subject matter, symbols, and ideas to communicate meaning

Reflecting Upon and Assessing the Characteristics and Merits of Their Work and the Work of Others

- Understands there are different responses to specific artworks

Suggested Vocabulary Words:

Accordion fold, torso, creature, imaginary

Materials Needed:

6-inch by 18-inch drawing paper

Colored markers or pencils

Procedure:

1. Have children fold paper in half lengthwise.
2. Fold in half again (lengthwise). There should be four sections.
3. In the first section, have a child draw the head of a person, animal, or imaginary creature.
4. After this is done, fold it over so that this section is hidden. Have the child pass the paper to the person beside him or her.
5. In the next section of the paper, have the child draw the torso of a person, animal, or creature.
6. After this is done, fold it over so that this section is hidden. Have the child pass the paper to the person beside him or her.
7. In the next section, have the child draw the legs of a person, animal, or creature.
8. After this is done, fold it over so that this section is hidden. Have the child pass the paper to the person beside him or her.
9. In the last section, have the child draw the feet of a person, animal, or creature.
10. When done, open up the folded drawing to reveal all of the sections. Give the drawing to the child who drew the head.
11. Have that child come up with a name for the creature.
12. Have the child write a story about the creature. Provide story starters such as: What is its name? Where does it live? What does it do for fun?
13. Have children share their stories when they have finished writing them.

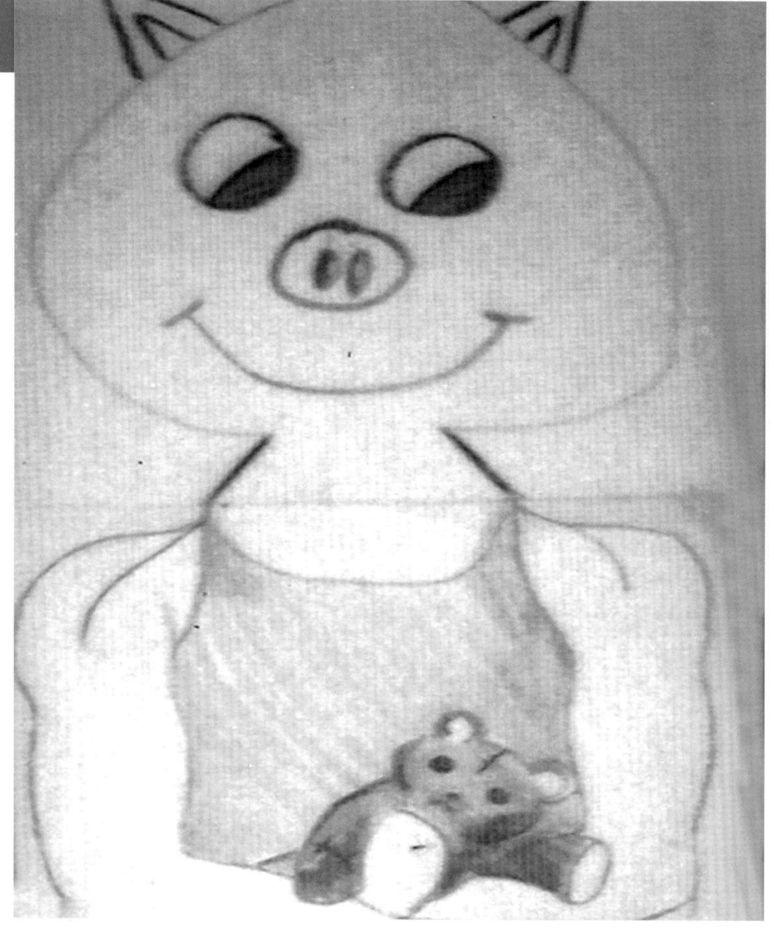

Table 4.10 Literacy Skills Nurtured in Crazy Creature Activity

Visual Perception & Discrimination	Sequencing	Language Acquisition	Fine Motor	Gross Motor	Hand-Eye Coordination	Critical Thinking
	●		●		●	●

What Children Will Learn:

- **Follow directions**—Folding paper correctly.
- **Critical thinking skills**—Creating the creatures and writing their stories.
- **Hand-eye coordination and fine motor skills**—Drawing and writing about the creature.
- **Sequencing skills**—Writing a story.

Game 1: Puppets in a Painting

Language Art Benchmarks:

Listening and Speaking Standard 8 (Level 1)

- Makes contributions in class and group discussions (e.g., reports on ideas and personal knowledge about a topic, initiates conversations, connects ideas and experiences with those of others)
- Asks and responds to questions (e.g., about the meaning of a story, about the meaning of words or ideas)
- Follows rules of conversation and group discussion (e.g., takes turns, raises hand to speak, stays on topic, focuses attention on speaker)
- Uses different voice level, phrasing, and intonation for different situations (e.g., small group settings, informal discussions, reports to the class)
- Uses level-appropriate vocabulary in speech (e.g., number words; words that describe people, places, things, events, location, actions; synonyms, antonyms; homonyms, word analogies, common figures of speech)
- Recites and responds to familiar stories, poems, and rhymes with patterns (e.g., relates information to own life; describes character, setting, plot)

Viewing Standard 9 (Level 1)

- Knows how different elements help to establish plot, setting, and character in visual narratives (e.g., action, dialogue, music, clothing, facial expressions)
- Knows different features (e.g., facial expressions, body language, gesture, clothing, actions, relationships, dialogue) that affect a viewer's perceptions of characters in visual media (e.g., qualities that identify a "hero" or a "villain")

Materials Needed:

Reproductions of a variety of artwork
Scissors
Glue
Tongue depressor
Masking tape

Procedure:

Cut out only the people portrayed in a variety of painting reproductions. Glue a tongue depressor on the back of each to make a puppet. Display a variety of landscape, cityscape, and seascape paintings around the room. Have each child take a puppet and choose the painting scene to serve as the backdrop. Children should be given time to write a puppet play for their character within the background scenery. They can then make their puppets talk to tell a story in their chosen environment. It is more interesting if characters from different paintings congregate in front of another painting to have a conversation. For example, what would the *American Gothic* (by Grant Wood) couple say to *Jacques and Berthe Lipchitz* (by Modigliani) if they were at the beach as portrayed in a seascape by Turner? This is a wonderful way to encourage children to interpret their characters. After this game is played, show the children the characters in their original painting.

Suggested Vocabulary Words:

Encourage children to use their own acquired vocabulary for this experience.

What Children Will Learn:

- **Visual perception**—Studying the painting backdrop to look for clues to tell a story with their puppet.
- **Sequencing, language, and critical thinking**—Writing the story and having their puppet(s) act it out.

National Visual Arts Standards:

Using Knowledge of Structures and Functions

- Knows the differences among visual characteristics and purposes of art in order to convey ideas
- Describes how different expressive features and organizational principles cause different responses
- Uses visual structures and functions of art to communicate ideas

Choosing and Evaluating a Range of Subject Matter, Symbols, and Ideas

- Selects and uses subject matter, symbols, and ideas to communicate meaning

Reflecting Upon and Assessing the Characteristics and Merits of Their Work and the Work of Others

- Understands there are different responses to specific artworks

Table 4.11 Literacy Skills Nurtured in Puppets in a Painting Game

Visual Perception & Discrimination	Sequencing	Language Acquisition	Fine Motor	Gross Motor	Hand-Eye Coordination	Critical Thinking
●	●	●				●

Game 2: Etch A Sketch® Game

Language Art Benchmarks:

Viewing Standard 9 (Level 1)

- Understands the main idea or message in visual media (e.g., pictures, cartoons, weather reports on television, newspaper photographs, visual narratives)

National Visual Arts Standards:

Understanding and Applying Media, Techniques, and Processes

- Knows the difference between materials and techniques
- Uses different media, techniques, and processes to communicate ideas, experiences, and stories
- Uses art materials and tools in a safe and responsible manner

Suggested Vocabulary Words:

Etch A Sketch®, horizontal, vertical

Materials Needed:

Etch A Sketch® (made by Ohio Art)

Plastic acetate sheets

Reproduction of artworks

Procedure:

Provide one Etch A Sketch for each group of three children. Prepare a transparent overlay to fit the screen of each Etch A Sketch. On this transparent overlay, write simple instructions for a child to draw a particular linear pattern (sample pattern provided by the adult) using the Etch A Sketch. After the lines are replicated by the children, they can view selected artworks to find lines similar to ones they have made on their Etch A Sketch.

What Children Will Learn:

- **Visual discrimination, fine motor skills and hand-eye coordination—** Drawing with the Etch A Sketch.
- **Critical thinking and language skills—** Scanning artworks to find linear patterns that are similar to the ones they have made on the Etch A Sketch. Talking about and describing how the lines can be used to make patterns or become a part of a more complex pattern.

Table 4.12 Literacy Skills Nurtured in Etch A Sketch® Game

Visual Perception & Discrimination	Sequencing	Language Acquisition	Fine Motor	Gross Motor	Hand-Eye Coordination	Critical Thinking
●		●	●		●	●

Game 3: News Reporter Game

Language Art Benchmarks:

Writing Standard 4 (Level 1)

- Uses a variety of sources to gather information (e.g., informational books, pictures, charts, indexes, videos, television programs, guest speakers, Internet, own observation)

Reading Standard 5 (Level 1)

- Uses meaning clues (e.g., picture captions, title, cover, headings, story structure, story topic) to aid comprehension and make predictions about content (e.g., action, events, character's behavior)

Reading Standard 6 (Level 1)

- Knows the main ideas or theme of a story

National Visual Arts Standards:

Using Knowledge of Structures and Functions

- Knows the differences among visual characteristics and purposes of art in order to convey ideas
- Describes how different expressive features and organizational principles cause different responses
- Uses visual structures and functions of art to communicate ideas

Choosing and Evaluating a Range of Subject Matter, Symbols, and Ideas

- Selects and uses subject matter, symbols, and ideas to communicate meaning

Reflecting Upon and Assessing the Characteristics and Merits of Their Work and the Work of Others

- Understands there are different responses to specific artworks

Materials Needed:

Cardboard tubes

Styrofoam balls (approximately 1½ inches)

Glue

Variety of artworks

Black or gray spray paint

Procedure:

Make a microphone by gluing a Styrofoam ball to the end of a cardboard tube. Spray-paint black or gray if desired. Select a variety of painting reproductions to display in your classroom or take the children to a museum. Divide children into groups of three and have each group select a painting as their focus. Have children pretend that they are news reporters and allow them time to look at their chosen artwork to get ideas for a news broadcast. Using their microphone, each group takes turns providing their newscast as they stand in front of their chosen painting and pretend they are on the scene of a news event.

Suggested Vocabulary Words:

Encourage children to use their own acquired vocabulary for this experience.

What Children Will Learn:

- **Visual perception skills**—Looking for clues in the artwork to tell their story.
- **Critical thinking and language**—Giving their news report.

Table 4.13 Literacy Skills Nurtured in the News Reporter Game

Visual Perception & Discrimination	Sequencing	Language Acquisition	Fine Motor	Gross Motor	Hand-Eye Coordination	Critical Thinking
●		●				●

Summary

This phase encompasses complex thinking that a child integrates into their artmaking experiences. The key milestones that emerge in this phase include:

- More detailed drawings
- More order in their drawings
- Portrayal of realism (in some cultures) in their artwork, which parallels their need at this age for realistic play experiences, such as having menus when playing restaurant
- More formal text that accompanies a drawing or work of art to communicate a story

"When children want to express more with their writing than labels and captions for drawings, the act of drawing itself provides a useful scaffold to story writing. Drawing helps children organize their ideas for expression in story writing in several ways" (Baghban 2007, p. 23). Therefore, encouraging drawing experiences for children can significantly benefit writing development. However, other art experiences can nurture the writing process, as explored in this chapter and the previous ones.

As a summary, the chart here demonstrates the phases of emergent writing as it relates to drawing. Keep in mind that children vary according to such factors as the amount of time spent with a proficient language user, exposure to books and various print materials, opportunities to read, and exposure to an environment that includes pictures and print.

Table 4.14 Progression of Writing and Drawing Development

Drawing/Writing Phase	Likely Actions
Observation of writing and drawing by others	Develops an idea that writing tools can mark surfaces.
Irregular scribbling	Uses writing tools to mark paper, walls, windows, etc.
Localized scribbling	Distinguishes the appropriate surfaces for making marks. Makes no pattern when scribbling on paper; understands that people make marks meaningfully.
Organized scribbling	Scribbles in controlled patterns, most often large congested circles or small separate circles.
Scribble Stories	Asks "What did I write?" "What did I draw?" and starts to name artistic creations.
Drawing and writing understood as separate processes	Can produce a specific letter or object on request.
Production of own name	Writes a version of his or her name. From this, begins to understand the alphabet.
Linear expansions	Makes wavy lines in either direction to fill in forms, writes grocery lists, tells stories; begins to include letter with the lines.
Labeling or captioning drawings	Writes and draws on the same page.
Prephonetic spelling	Writes according to how words sound; uses sounding out to choose consonants, occasionally attempts vowels.
Drawing as inspiration or help for longer stories	Writes, stops to draw on separate paper, returns to the story.
Writing long stories	Writes stories, rarely illustrated, with more conventional spellings; becomes a visual speller through reading.

This table is adapted from Baghban (2007, p.25)

Celebrating Children's Art and Literacy Experiences: Final Thoughts and Connections

The Art and Literacy Connection Revisited

In the previous chapters, we presented ways that the visual arts develop early literacy skills in young children. We wanted to give parents and teachers easy and manageable experiences to effectively engage their children. The experiences themselves can be viewed as early attempts at fostering language and literacy skills. In these experiences children are given opportunities to construct their ideas through the visual arts. They are putting into their artistic creations what they are thinking and feeling at that moment. However, instead of using words, they are using images and visual symbols to tell their stories, experiences, and understanding of the world.

In this final chapter, we summarize the connection between visual art and literacy, explore ways that art can be displayed and reflected upon, and discuss how to talk to young children about their artworks and art projects.

Scribbles are the first graphic marks babies make for kinesthetic pleasure. Although they are the first signs of literacy development, these early markings are not a representation of thought or emotion. Authentic early writing begins when a child intentionally picks up a marking tool and creates marks on a surface. These markings and drawings are children's attempts to tell us what they know, what they think, and how they think about a particular subject. "When a teacher invites children to write and some children draw, it is important that the teacher treat the drawings as writings until the children tell the teacher that they are not" (Baghban 2007, p. 24). As children get older, they begin to replace the symbols they use in their artworks with conventional writing symbols in the form of letters and numbers.

The art that children create is in itself a working language as it tells us what the child knows or is trying to say, without using words. The different materials that children begin to use become distinct languages in their own right. Clay becomes a language, paper and markers become another language, while paper and scissors become yet another. Children use these

When a teacher invites children to write and some children draw, it is important that the teacher treat the drawings as writings until the children tell the teacher that they are not.

(Baghban, 2007)

distinct languages to share what they know or have experienced. Young children do not have the ability to verbalize their stories, but have an uncanny ability to tell their stories visually in great detail through their artwork. For example, think about a child who can tell a brief story about a princess, but once asked to draw that story on paper, a rich dialogue emerges (see picture 5.1 and story for an example). It's not that the child has learned anything new about princesses, but rather that the child is now using the drawing or art experience as a vehicle to tell the story. The picture or artistic creation triggers other experiences children may want to share. Sometimes a small mark on a paper may actually be a story in itself. It may be difficult for children to remember the stories, but once on paper, their markings can be used to revisit and retell their experiences. This is why we often see few marks on a child's paper, but we hear a rich and interesting story.

The drawing experience is a process of self-expression and communication and not always one of representation. Young children are not skilled at object representation and often create lines or shapes that are difficult for adults to decipher. For instance, a child trying to draw a telephone may simply draw a box, but when they tell their story they call the box a telephone.

Children's graphic expressions in the early years focus on the exploration of the materials they are given to use. How they use those materials to create artworks becomes a language. Thus, telling stories and putting thoughts on paper or into an artwork, no matter how abstract and illegible this work appears to adults, are for children the first steps in using literacy to explain themselves and show what they know.

As children get older, they begin to infuse words into their drawings (Dyson, 1993). We begin to see a picture with the child's name on it or we may see a picture with a few letters, a child's early attempt at writing. As children move into the upper elementary grades, they may no longer depend on the picture to tell their story or idea and may begin to use more conventional writing symbols or oral language to tell us what they think or know. However, the mental picture never disappears and is still used as an impetus for their story writing. In fact, children will write better with a visual referent.

Now that children have created all these wonderful visual images and stories, it is important to provide opportunities for them to revisit these works. One way to do that is by displaying children's art in the home or classroom where it is clearly visible.

When once upon a time there was a little boy named Jacob. And then his mom had a little sister. And then some rain dropped on him. And they lived in a big chair. And Jacob needed to go to school. And he did not like his school. But at school the next day some rain dropped on Jacob, on his hair. There was grass. Then Jacob could not get on the grass. He had shoes, magic shoes, to match the grass. And then his sister got magic shoes too, little tiny ones. And they loved their new house. And they lived happily ever after.

Jordan, age 4

Picture 5.1

Displaying Children's Artworks

An important thing to remember when displaying children's artwork is to hang it or set it up at the child's eye level and not that of an adult. This way the child can fully view the artwork. While displaying the artwork, we must be aware of the importance of text that accompanies the work. We should take care to include the child's story alongside the artwork to allow a better understanding of the child's intent during the creative process. The text can be written by the child or by an adult to document the learning process. Teachers who want to show parents what children are learning through their artwork could highlight the learning standards being met. This will further demonstrate to the viewer the quality of the experience as well as the presence of a clear learning outcome.

Consider changing artworks regularly. As teachers and parents, we often keep the same pictures or projects up for weeks, months, and some of us for the entire year! Although there is no timetable for how long art should be displayed in early childhood classrooms, it is a good idea to replace projects once the children are no longer engaged with them (that is, not looking at them or discussing them). Display new artworks on topics of interest to children or works they have recently completed as part of a lesson or ongoing unit. Avoid displaying artworks children are currently working on because they will revisit them frequently to continue their work. For artworks in progress, find a space where children can safely leave their work so that others can view them and learn the process that is being undertaken and the topic explored.

The cost of attractively displaying art can be minimal. Children can be taught to create their own borders or frames. Inexpensive frames can be purchased at most office or craft stores for about $5 to $20, depending on size. The frames add a nice touch and express to children that their work is valued.

Children take pride in putting their names on their artworks. These signatures make the artworks easily identifiable for parents, teachers, and peers. Once in a while, though, try to exclude names on the pictures so that visitors and peers can learn to enjoy the works of all children and not seek out specific ones.

Once the work is taken out of the frame or your display case, children should be permitted to take it home. Children who choose not to take their artwork home should be allowed to decide what to do with it. The teacher may invite the child to recycle the work or donate it to another child or other people, such as the principal, local retailers, or relatives. Other children may choose to reuse some of the materials in a new project they are working on or recycle materials that could be reused later. Whatever they choose, children should be allowed to decide what to do with their artwork after it is taken down, if possible.

Reflecting and Revisiting

When we display children's artwork, we are giving them an opportunity to reflect on and revisit the work. In doing so, children begin to understand how they see the world in comparison to how others (adults and children) see it. Furthermore, children can begin to revise their own hypotheses as they revisit and rethink what is on display. Children may even create a new rendition of the artwork based on new ideas and hypotheses they have developed after revisiting their work or the work of their peers (Edwards, Gandini & Forman, 1998).

To allow children to engage in this process, we must leave artworks on display for the right amount of time. Earlier we stated that there is no set time for how long artworks should be displayed, but if you see children still using the artworks to rethink ideas, the works should stay up. If children are no longer reflecting or visiting the artworks and are not using them as a springboard to other experiences, consider taking them down and replacing them with new works. Try to provide enough time for children to fully experience the works on display and to use them to rethink their own beliefs and ideas.

Talking About Art

When talking to children about their art and art projects, we must remember to be respectful of the work and the children. Below are some suggestions for talking to children about their artworks:

- Never presume that you know what the artwork is about.
- Be respectful by asking the child to tell you about his or her work. This will encourage language development and may evolve into an exciting dialogue between you and the child.
- If a child is having difficulty talking about his or her work, you can serve as a facilitator by directing the child to look at the colors used, variety of lines visible, and other properties of the work to spark conversation. This is a great opportunity for you to introduce new vocabulary words to the child.
- Use developmentally appropriate language that the child can easily understand.
- If the child is nonverbal, you can still talk to the child about his or her artwork, pointing out specific characteristics such as colors, lines, and shapes as you describe each one.
- Talking to children about their artwork is essential because conversation stimulates language acquisition and helps the child begin the process of telling stories.

Art Auctions

One way to make children feel like real artists is to hold an art auction. These can be held on a weekly, monthly, or yearly basis. Ask children to donate their artworks to the class and then have them auctioned off at a school event. Invite parents to the auction to view and bid on children's artworks. For schools or programs that have a hard time getting parents to participate, this event may draw them into the school. The proceeds from the auction sales can go toward the purchase of equipment or supplies for the school or classroom. Consider inviting members of the community, especially if this is a schoolwide event. The school could host a preview of all works of art and an auction would follow. Children could be encouraged to auction off their own artworks. This wonderful oral language experience requires children to use descriptive vocabulary to talk about their works and entice people to buy them. Remember not to price anything too high! You want all works to sell! The goal is not to make money, but to empower children and get parents to participate in a classroom or school event.

Making Art Accessible Today

Many schools are putting aside the visual arts to focus on academic subjects such as math and science. Without question, those subjects are of major importance and need to be well taught. However, with a higher emphasis on academics and a "pushing down" of curriculum on younger children (for example, bringing 1st grade curriculum into the kindergarten classroom), the creative experiences that children need to grow and develop have been taken away. With many schools excluding the visual arts, parents must learn how they can incorporate these experiences in their own homes. Also, educators must rethink how they can use the visual arts (perhaps through an integrative approach) to help better teach children the academic subjects. Connecting academic standards (for science, math, and literacy) to children's art experiences is an easy way to not only integrate curriculum, but also to show administrators how standards are being addressed through art. Because art is a natural form of expression for children, we must embrace it as a meaningful way to teach children how to think and construct knowledge. We are challenging parents and educators to not lose sight of the powerful influence that the visual arts can have on their children's development.

See Appendix C for Children's Book Resources.

Daddy
age: 28
Mommy
age: 28
Paige
age: 10
Aiden
age: 5

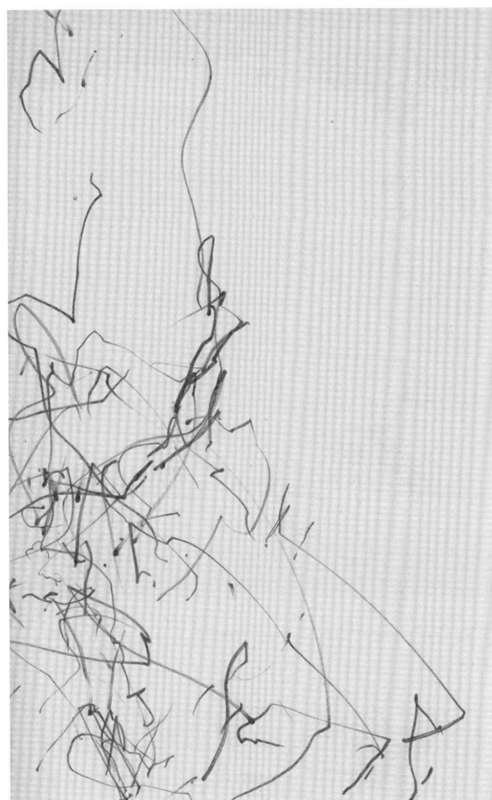

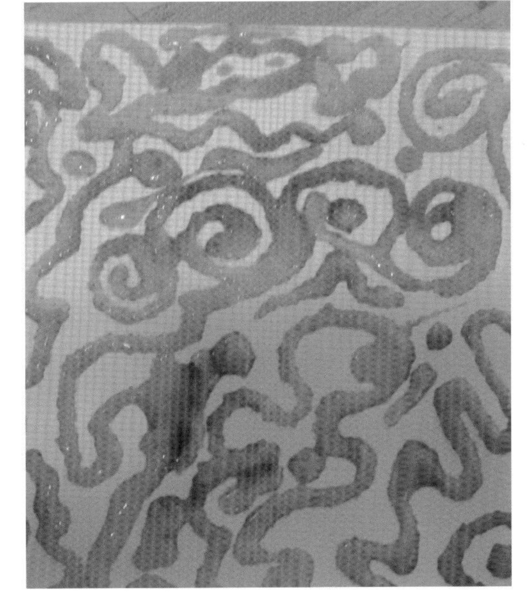

Book References & Appendixes

Book References

Alexander, R. J. (1992). *Policy and practice in primary education.* London: Routledge.

Allen, K. E., & Marotz, L. R. (2007). *Developmental profiles: Pre-birth through twelve.* Clifton Park, NY: Thomson Delmar Learning.

Anning, A. (1997). Drawing out ideas: Graphicacy and young children. *International Journal of Technology and Design Education, 7*(3), 219-239.

Applebee, A. N. (1978). *The child's concept of story: Ages two to seventeen*. Chicago: University of Chicago Press.

April, A. (2001). Toward a final description of the connection between arts education and student achievement. *Arts Education Policy Review, 102*(5), 25-26.

Baghban, M. (2007). Scribbles, labels, and stories: The role of drawing in the development of writing. *Young Children, 62*(1), 20-26.

Barrs, M. (1988). Drawing a story: Transitions between drawing and writing. In M. Lightfoot & N. Martin (Eds.), *The word for teaching is learning: Essays for James Britton.* Portsmouth, NH: Heinemann.

Bergen, D. ,& Coscia, J. (2001) *Brain research and childhood education: Implications for teaching.* Olney, MD: Association for Childhood Education International.

Bland, J.C. (1957) *Art of the young child.* New York: Museum of Modern Art.

Braswell, G., & Callanan, M. A. (2003). Learning to draw recognizable graphic representations during mother-child interactions. *Merrill-Palmer Quarterly, 49*(4), 471-494.

Catterall, J. S. (1998). Involvement in the arts and success in the secondary school. Washington, DC: Americans for the Arts Monograph Series, Vol. 1 No. 9.

Chapman, L. (1978). *Approaches to art education.* New York: Harcourt Brace Jovanovich.

Clay, M. (1995) *What did I write? Beginning writing behaviour.* Portsmouth, NH: Heinemann.

Cole, E., & Schaefer, C. (1990). Can young children be art critics? *Young Children, 45*(2), 33-38.

Cole, L. (1994). Activating aesthetic dialog with young children: A multi-response approach. *Ohio Art Education Association Journal, 32*(2), 12-20.

Cooper-Solomon, D. (1995). The arts are essential. *School Arts, 94*(6), 29-30.

Dietrich, G., & Hunnicut, C. (1948). Art content preferred by primary grade children. *Elementary School Journal, 48*(10), 557-559.

Douglas, N., Schwartz, J. & Taylor, J.B. (1981). The relationship of cognitive style of young children and their modes of responding to paintings. *Studies in Art Education, 22*(3), 24-31.

Dyson, A. H. (1993). *Social worlds of children learning to write in an urban primary school.* New York: Teachers College Press.

Edwards, C., Gandini, L., & Forman, G. (Eds.). (1998). *The hundred languages of children: The Reggio Emilia approach—Advanced reflections* (2nd ed.). Greenwich, CT: Ablex.

Efland, A. (2002). *Arts and cognition: Integrating the visual arts in the curriculum.* New York: Teachers College Press.

Eglinton, K. A. (2003). *Art in the early years.* London: Routledge Falmer.

Eisner, E. W. (1972). *Educating artistic vision.* New York: Collier Macmillan.

Eisner, E. W. (1976). *The arts, human development, and education.* Berkeley, CA: McCutchan Publishing Corp.

Eisner, E. W. (1988). *The role of discipline-based art education in America's schools.* Los Angeles: Getty Education Institute for the Arts.

Eisner, E. W. (1991). *The enlightened eye: Qualitative inquiry and the enhancement of educational practice.* New York: Macmillan Publishing Co.

Eisner, E. W. (2002). *The arts and the creation of mind.* New Haven, CT: Yale University Press.

Engel, B. S. (2002). *Considering children's art: Why and how to value their works* (2nd printing). Washington, DC: National Association for the Education of Young Children.

Epstein, A. S. (2001) Thinking about art: Encouraging art appreciation in early childhood settings. *Young Children, 56*(3), 38-43.

Epstein, A. S., & Trimis, E. (2002). *Supporting young artists: The development of the visual arts in young children.* Ypsilanti, MI: High Scope Press.

Feldman, E. B. (1985). *Thinking about art.* Englewood Cliffs, NJ: Prentice-Hall.

Froebel, F. (1974). *The education of man.* Clifton, NJ: Augustus M. Kelley Publishers.

Fiske, E. B. (Ed.) (1999). *Champions of change: The impact of the arts on learning.* Washington, DC: Arts Education Partnership and the President's Committee on the Arts and Humanities.

Gardner, H., & Winner, E. (1976, March). How children learn: Three stages of understanding art. *Psychology Today, 9,* 42-43.

Gardner, H. (1980). *Artful scribbles.* New York: Basic Books.

Gardner, H. (1983). *Frames of mind: The theory of multiple intelligences.* New York: Basic Books.

Genishi, C., & Dyson, A. H. (1984). *Language assessment in the early years.* Norwood, NJ: Ablex Publishing.

Goldhawk, S. (1998). *Young children and the arts: Making creative connections.* Washington, DC: Arts Education Partnership.

Hardiman, G. W., & Zernich, T. (1977). Influence of style and subject matter on the development of children's art preferences. *Studies in Art Education, 19*(1), 29-35.

Hardiman, G. W., & Zernich, T. (1982). The relative influence of parts and wholes in shaping preference responses to paintings. *Studies in Art Education, 23*(3), 31-38.

Harste, J. C., & Burke, C . L., Woodward, V.A. (1984). *Language stories and literacy lessons.* Portsmouth, NH: Heinemann.

Hart, L. (1993). The role of cultural context in multicultural aesthetics. *Journal of Multicultural and Cross-cultural Research in Art Education, 10/11*(1), 5-19.

Howe, K. R. (1997). *Understanding equal educational opportunity: Social justice, democracy, and schooling.* New York: Teachers College Press.

Hudson, W. (1960). Pictorial depth perception in sub-cultural groups in Africa. *The Journal of Social Psychology, 52,* 183-208.

Hurwitz, A., & Day, M. (1991) *Children and their art: Methods for the elementary school* (5th ed.). New York: Harcourt Brace Jovanovich.

Jalongo, M. R. (2004). *Young children and picture books* (2nd ed.). Washington, DC: National Association for the Education of Young Children.

Kellogg, R. (1970). *Analyzing children's art.* Palo Alto, CA: Mayfield Publishing Company.

Kerlavage, M. S. (1995). A bunch of naked ladies and a tiger: Children's responses to adult works of art. In C.M. Thompson (Ed.), *The visual arts and early childhood Learning* (p. 56-62). Reston, VA: National Art Education Association.

Kindler, A. M., Darras, B. (1994). Artistic development in context: Emergence and development of pictorial imagery in the early childhood years. *Visual Arts Research, 20*(2), 1-13.

Kindler, A. M., & Thompson, C. (1994, April). Social interactions and young children's artistic learning. Paper presented at the National Art Education Association Convention, Baltimore, MD.

Kindler, A. M. (Ed.). (1997). *Child development in art.* Reston, VA: National Art Education Association.

Kolbe, U. (1997). *Clay and children: More than making pots.* Canberra, Australia: Australian Early Childhood Association Resource Book Series.

Kolbe, U. (2005). *It's not a bird yet: The drama of drawing.* Byron Bay, Australia: Peppinot Press.

Lanier, V. (1982). *The arts we see.* New York: Teachers College Press.

Lewis, H. (1982). Tools and tasks, the place of developmental studies: An open letter to Brent and Marjorie Wilson. *Art Education, 35*(3), 8-9.

Lewis, D. (2001). *Reading contemporary picturebooks: picturing text.* London: Routledge Falmer.

Lowenfeld, V., & Brittain, W. (1987). *Creative and mental growth.* New York: Macmillan Publishers.

Machotka, P. (1966). Aesthetic criteria in childhood: Justifications of preference. *Child Development, 37,* 877-885.

Malaguzzi, L. (1998). History, ideas, and basic philosophy of Reggio Emilia: An interview with Lella Gandini. In C. Edwards, L. Gandini, G. Forman (Eds.), *The hundred languages of children: The Reggio Emilia approach—Advanced reflections* (2nd edition). Greenwich, CT: Ablex.

Mayer, K. (2007). Emerging knowledge about emergent writing. *Young Children, 62*(1), 34-40.

McFee, J., & Degge, R. (1980). *Art, culture, and environment.* Dubuque, IA: Kendall/Hunt Publishing Company.

Mid-continent Research for Education and Learning (2006). Language arts standards. Retrieved August 29, 2006, from http://www.mcrel.org/compendium/SubjectTopics.asp?SubjectID=7.

Mortimore, P., Sammons, P., Stoll, L., Lewis, D., & Ecob, R. (1988). *School matters: The junior years.* London: Open Books.

Mundy-Castle, A.C. (1966). Pictorial depth perception in Ghanaian children. *International Journal of Psychology, 1,* 289-301.

National Assessment of Educational Progress. (2001). *The nation's report card.* Retrieved March 23, 2007, from http://nces.ed.gov/nationsreportcard/.

Neuman, S., Copple, C., & Bredekamp, S. (2000). *Learning to read and write: Developmentally appropriate practices or young children.* Washington, DC: National Association for the Education of Young Children.

Newton, C. (1995). Language and learning about art. In Thompson, C. (Ed.), *The visual arts and early childhood learning.* Reston, VA: National Art Education Association.

Newton, C. & Kantner, L. (1977). Cross-cultural research in aesthetic development: A review. In Kindler, A. (Ed). *Child development in art.* Reston, VA: National Art Education Association.

Olshansky, B. (1995). Picture this: An arts-based literature program. *Educational Leadership, 53*(1), 44-47.

Parsons, M. (1987). *How we understand art: A cognitive development account of aesthetic experiences.* Cambridge, UK: Cambridge University Press.

Richards, A. J. (1988). Perceptual training in drawing among students from two countries. *Studies in Art Education, 29*(3), 302-308.

Schaefer, C. L. (1999) *The squiggle.* New York: Dragonfly Books.

Schirrmacher, R. (1998) *Art and creative development for young children.* Clifton Park, NY: Thomson Delmar Learning.

Shaffer, S. ,& Danko-McGhee, K. (2004, Fall). *Looking at art with toddlers, NAEA Advisory.* Reston, VA: National Art Education Association.

Sheridan, S. R. (2002). Drawing/writing. Retrieved November 1, 2006, from http://www.drawingwriting.com.

Sigel, I. E. (1984). A constructivist perspective for teaching thinking: A distancing strategy model. *Educational Leadership, 42*(3), 18-21.

Steele, B. (1998) *Draw me a story.* Winnipeg, Manitoba: Peguis Publishers.

Stokrocki, M. (1984). The meaning of aesthetic awareness for preschoolers in a museum class. *Art Education, 37*(2), 12-16.

Taunton, M. (1980). The influence of age on preferences for subject matter, realism, and spatial depth in painting reproductions. *Studies in Art Education, 21*(3), 40-53.

Temple, C., Nathan, R., & Burris, N. (1982). *The beginnings of writing.* Boston: Allyn & Bacon.

Thompson, C., & Bales, S. (1991). Michael doesn't like my dinosaurs: Conversations in a preschool art class. *Studies in Art Education, 33,* 43-45.

Tizard, B., Blatchford, P., Burke, J., Farguar, C. & Plewis, I. (1988). *Young children at school in the inner city.* Hove, UK: Lawrence Erlbaum Associates.

UNESCO (2007). Literacy. Retrieved July 27, 2007 from http://portal.unesco.org/education/en/ev.php-URL_ID=40338&URL_DO=DO_TOPIC&URL_SECTION=201.html

Vygotsky, L. S. (1978). Mind in society: *The development of higher psychological processes.* Cambridge, MA: Harvard University Press.

Wachowiak, F., & Clements, R. (2006) *Emphasis art: A qualitative art program for elementary and middle schools.* New York: Pearson Education.

Wilson, B., & Wilson, M. (1981) The use and uselessness of developmental stages. *Art Education, 34*(5), 4-5.

Zepeda-de-Kane, F. P. (1980). *Young children's drawings as related to basic communication skills.* Monograph #31. P.K. Younger Laboratory School, University of Florida.

Zulasky, V.L. (1982). What did I write? What did I draw? In W. Frawley (Ed.), *Linguistics and literacy.* New York: Plenum.

Appendix A

Mid-continent Research for Education and Learning

List of Benchmarks for Language Arts

http://www.mcrel.org/compendium/SubjectTopics.asp?SubjectID=7

Retrieved 9/4/06

Writing Standard 1

Uses the general skills and strategies of the writing process

Level Pre-K (Grades Pre-K)

1. Knows that writing, including pictures, letters, and words, communicates meaning and information
2. Uses drawings to express thoughts, feelings, and ideas
3. Uses forms of emergent writing (e.g., scribble writing, random symbols, random letter-like marks) to represent ideas
4. Dictates stories, poems, and personal narratives
5. Uses emergent writing skills to write for a variety of purposes (e.g., to make lists, to send messages, to write stories) and to write in a variety of forms (e.g., journals, sign-in sheets, name cards, cards with words and pictures)
6. Uses knowledge of letters to write or copy familiar words, such as own name
7. Uses writing tools and materials (e.g., pencils, crayons, chalk, markers, rubber stamps, computers, paper, cardboard, chalkboard)

Level I (Grades K-2)

1. Prewriting: Uses prewriting strategies to plan written work (e.g., discusses ideas with peers, draws pictures to generate ideas, writes key thoughts and questions, rehearses ideas, records reactions and observations)
2. Drafting and revising: Uses strategies to draft and revise written work (e.g., rereads; rearranges words, sentences, and paragraphs to improve or clarify meaning; varies sentence type; adds descriptive words and details; deletes extraneous information; incorporates suggestions from peers and teachers; sharpens the focus)
3. Editing and publishing: Uses strategies to edit and publish written work (e.g., proofreads using a dictionary and other resources; edits for grammar, punctuation, capitalization, and spelling at a developmentally appropriate level; incorporates illustrations or photos; uses available, appropriate technology to compose and publish work; shares finished product)
4. Evaluates own and others' writing (e.g., asks questions and makes comments about writing, helps classmates apply grammatical and mechanical conventions)
5. Uses strategies to organize written work (e.g., includes a beginning, middle, and ending; uses a sequence of events)
6. Uses writing and other methods (e.g., using letters or phonetically spelled words, telling, dictating, making lists) to describe familiar persons, places, objects, or experiences
7. Writes in a variety of forms or genres (e.g., picture books, friendly letters, stories, poems, information pieces, invitations, personal experience narratives, messages, responses to literature)
8. Writes for different purposes (e.g., to entertain, inform, learn, communicate ideas)

Writing Standard 2

Uses the stylistic and rhetorical aspects of writing

Level Pre-K (Grades Pre-K)

1. Not appropriate for this level

Level I (Grades K-2)

1. Uses descriptive words to convey basic ideas
2. Uses declarative and interrogative sentences in written compositions

Writing Standard 3

Uses grammatical and mechanical conventions in written compositions

Level Pre-K (Grades Pre-K)

1. Applies rudimentary rules of grammar
2. Uses phonic knowledge to spell simple words

Level I (Grades K-2)

1. Uses conventions of print in writing (e.g., forms letters in print, uses upper- and lowercase letters of the alphabet, spaces words and sentences, writes from left-to-right and top-to-bottom, includes margins
2. Uses complete sentences in written compositions
3. Uses nouns in written compositions (e.g., nouns for simple objects, family members, community workers, and categories)
4. Uses verbs in written compositions (e.g., verbs for a variety of situations, action words)
5. Uses adjectives in written compositions (e.g., uses descriptive words)
6. Uses adverbs in written compositions (i.e., uses words that answer how, when, where, and why questions)
7. Uses conventions of spelling in written compositions (e.g., spells high frequency, commonly misspelled words from appropriate grade-level list; spells phonetically regular words; uses letter-sound relationships; spells basic short vowel, long vowel, r-controlled, and consonant blend patterns; uses a dictionary and other resources to spell words)
8. Uses conventions of capitalization in written compositions (e.g., first and last names, first word of a sentence)
9. Uses conventions of punctuation in written compositions (e.g., uses periods after declarative sentences, uses questions marks after interrogative sentences, uses commas in a series of words)

Writing Standard 4
Gathers and uses information for research purposes

Level Pre-K (Grades Pre-K)

1. Not appropriate for this level

Level I (Grades K-2)

1. Generates questions about topics of personal interest
2. Uses a variety of sources to gather information (e.g., informational books, pictures, charts, indexes, videos, television programs, guest speakers, Internet, own observation)

Reading Standard 5
Uses the general skills and strategies of the reading process

Level Pre-K (Grades Pre-K)

1. Knows that print and written symbols convey meaning and represent spoken language
2. Understands the differences between letters, numbers, and words and knows the significance of spaces between words
3. Understands that illustrations and pictures convey meaning
4. Knows the proper way to handle books (e.g., hold the book upright; turn pages from front to back, one at a time)
5. Knows that print is read from left to right, top to bottom, and that books are read front to back
6. Knows some letters of the alphabet, such as those in the student's own name
7. Knows some familiar words in print, such as own first name
8. Knows that print appears in different forms (e.g., labels, letters, storybooks) and serves different purposes (e.g., to inform)
9. Knows familiar print in their environment (e.g., traffic signs, store logos)
10. Predicts story events or outcomes, using illustrations and prior knowledge as a guide
11. Uses emergent reading skills to "read" a story (e.g., gathers meaning from words and pictures)
12. Knows that books have titles, authors, and often illustrators
13. Uses visual and verbal cues, including pictures, to comprehend new words and stories

Level I (Grades K-2)

1. Uses mental images based on pictures and print to aid in comprehension of text
2. Uses meaning clues (e.g., picture captions, title, cover, headings, story structure, story topic) to aid comprehension and make predictions about content (e.g., action, events, character's behavior)
3. Uses basic elements of phonetic analysis (e.g., common letter/sound relationships, beginning and ending consonants, vowel sounds, blends, word patterns) to decode unknown words
4. Uses basic elements of structural analysis (e.g., syllables, basic prefixes, suffixes, root words, compound words, spelling patterns, contractions) to decode unknown words
5. Uses a picture dictionary to determine word meaning
6. Understands level-appropriate sight words and vocabulary (e.g., words for persons, places, things, actions; high frequency words such as said, was, and where)
7. Uses self-correction strategies (e.g., searches for cues, identifies miscues, rereads, asks for help)
8. Reads aloud familiar stories, poems, and passages with fluency and expression (e.g., rhythm, flow, meter, tempo, pitch, tone, intonation)

Reading Standard 6

Uses reading skills and strategies to understand and interpret a variety of literary texts

Level Pre-K (Grades Pre-K)

1. Knows the sequence of events (e.g., beginning, middle, and end) in a story
2. Knows the elements that compose a story (e.g., characters, plot, events, setting)
3. Understands the literal meaning of plays, poems, and stories
4. Knows the difference between fact and fiction, real and make-believe
5. Relates stories to his/her own life and experience

Level I (Grades K-2)

1. Uses reading skills and strategies to understand a variety of familiar literary passages and texts (e.g., fairy tales, folktales, fiction, nonfiction, legends, fables, myths, poems, nursery rhymes, picture books, predictable books)
2. Knows the basic characteristics of familiar genres (e.g., picture books, fairy tales, nursery rhymes)
3. Knows setting, main characters, main events, sequence, and problems in stories
4. Knows the main ideas or theme of a story
5. Relates stories to personal experiences (e.g., events, characters, conflicts, themes)

Reading Standard 7

Uses reading skills and strategies to understand and interpret a variety of informational texts

Level Pre-K (Grades Pre-K)

1. Not appropriate for this level

Level I (Grades K-2)

1. Uses reading skills and strategies to understand a variety of informational texts (e.g., written directions, signs, captions, warning labels, informational books)
2. Understands the main idea and supporting details of simple expository information
3. Summarizes information found in texts (e.g., retells in own words)
4. Relates new information to prior knowledge and experience

Listening and Speaking Standard 8

Uses listening and speaking strategies for different purposes

Level Pre-K (Grades Pre-K)

1. Speaks clearly enough to be understood by unfamiliar adults and uses appropriate levels of volume, tone, and inflection
2. Uses new vocabulary to describe feelings, thoughts, experiences, and observations
3. Speaks expressively (e.g., uses different voices for various characters)
4. Uses descriptive language (e.g., color words; size words, such as bigger, smaller; shape words)
5. Tells stories based on personal experience or make-believe
6. Asks questions to obtain information
7. Answers simple questions
8. Follows conversation rules (e.g., taking turns, making relevant comments; staying on topic) when talking with peers and adults
9. Creates or acts out familiar stories, songs, rhymes, and plays in play activities
10. Retells a story with attention to the sequence of main events
11. Listens for a variety of purposes (e.g., to gain and share information, to perform a task, for enjoyment, to learn what happened in a story, to converse with an adult or peer)
12. Understands messages in conversations (e.g. responds differently based on purpose of messages in conversation; attends and responds to conversations)
13. Follows one- and two-step directions
14. Understands basic conversational vocabulary
15. Discriminates among the sounds of spoken language

Listening and Speaking Standard 8 (continued)

1. Knows rhyming sounds and simple rhymes (e.g., identifies rhymes and rhyming sounds)
2. Knows that words are made up of sounds (e.g., that words can begin alike, sound alike)
3. Knows that words are made up of syllables
4. Listens to a variety of fiction, nonfiction, poetry, drama, rhymes, and songs

Level I (Grades K-2)

1. Makes contributions in class and group discussions (e.g., reports on ideas and personal knowledge about a topic, initiates conversations, connects ideas and experiences with those of others)
2. Asks and responds to questions (e.g., about the meaning of a story, about the meaning of words or ideas)
3. Follows rules of conversation and group discussion (e.g., takes turns, raises hand to speak, stays on topic, focuses attention on speaker)
4. Uses different voice level, phrasing, and intonation for different situations (e.g., small group settings, informal discussions, reports to the class)
5. Uses level-appropriate vocabulary in speech (e.g., number words; words that describe people, places, things, events, location, actions; synonyms, antonyms; homonyms, word analogies, common figures of speech)
6. Gives and responds to oral directions
7. Recites and responds to familiar stories, poems, and rhymes with patterns (e.g., relates information to own life; describes character, setting, plot)
8. Knows differences between language used at home and language used in school

Viewing Standard 9
Uses viewing skills and strategies to understand and interpret visual media

Level Pre-K (Grades Pre-K)

1. Not appropriate for this level

Level I (Grades K-2)

1. Understands the main idea or message in visual media (e.g., pictures, cartoons, weather reports on television, newspaper photographs, visual narratives)
2. Uses a variety of strategies to predict content and meaning in visual media (e.g., uses knowledge of the structure of television programs: for cartoons, make predictions based on program length, experience that a resolution will be reached and that main characters will overcome difficulties to return to the next episode; uses knowledge of cause-and-effect relationships to predict plot development)
3. Knows how different elements help to establish plot, setting, and character in visual narratives (e.g., action, dialogue, music, clothing, facial expressions)
4. Knows different features (e.g., facial expressions, body language, gesture, clothing, actions, relationships, dialogue) that affect a viewer's perceptions of characters in visual media (e.g., qualities that identify a "hero" or a "villain")
5. Knows different elements from films, videos, television, and other visual media that appeal to him or her (e.g., scary parts, action segments, particular characters, color, sound effects, animation, layout, music)
6. Understands the similarities and differences between real life and life depicted in visual media (e.g., compares own family to families represented in television cartoons or films; knows that there is a difference between a character in a program and the actor)

Appendix B

National Visual Art Standards

http://www.kinderart.com/artspeak/standards.shtml

Retrieved 9/21/06

Understanding and Applying Media, Techniques and Processes

1. Know the difference between materials & techniques.
2. Describe how different materials, techniques, and processes cause different responses.
3. Use different media, techniques, and processes to communicate ideas, experiences, and stories.
4. Use art materials and tools in a safe and responsible manner.

Using Knowledge of Structures and Functions

1. Know the differences among visual characteristics and purposes of art in order to convey ideas.
2. Describe how different expressive features and organizational principles cause different responses.
3. Use visual structures and functions of art to communicate ideas.

Choosing and Evaluating a Range of Subject Matter Symbols and Ideas

1. Explore & understand prospective content for works of art.
2. Select & use subject matter, symbols, & ideas to communicate meaning.
3. Know the visual arts have both a history & specific relationships to various cultures.

Reflecting Upon and Assessing the Characteristics and Merits of their Work and the Work of Others

1. Understand there are various purposes for creating works of visual art.
2. Describe how people's experiences influence the development of specific artworks.
3. Understand there are different responses to specific artworks.

Making Connections between the Visual Arts and the Other Disciplines

1. Understand & use similarities & differences between characteristics of the visual arts & other arts disciplines.
2. Identify connections between the visual arts & other disciplines in the curriculum.

Appendix C

Children's Books and Art Resources

Books to Stimulate Babies' Visual Perception

Barnyard Banter by Denise Fleming (1994). New York: Henry Holt and Company.

Drummer Hoff by Barbara Emberley (1967). New York: Simon & Schuster Children's Publishing.

Mama Cat Has Three Kittens by Denise Fleming (1998). New York: Henry Holt and Company.

Shadow by Blaise Cendrars and Marcia Brown (illustrator) (1982). New York: Charles Scribner's Sons.

Thump-Thump-Rat-A-Tat-Tat by Gene Baer (1989). New York: Harper & Row.

Time to Sleep by Denise Fleming (1997). New York: Henry Holt and Company.

Where Once There Was a Wood by Denise Fleming (1996). New York: Henry Holt and Company.

Books About Clouds

Clouds by Henry Fountain (2004). New York: Barnes & Noble.

Cloud Dance by Thomas Locker (2000). New York: Harcourt.

I Call It Sky by Will C. Howell (1999). New York: Walker & Company.

It Looked Like Spilt Milk by Charles G. Shaw (1947). New York: Harper Collins Publishers.

Little Cloud by Eric Carle (1996). New York: Philomel Books.

Books About Color

A Rainbow of My Own by Don Freeman (1978). New York: Puffin Books.

Baby Einstein: Van Gogh's World of Color by Julie Aigner-Clark (2001). New York: Hyperion Books for Children.

Color Dance by Ann Jonas (1989). New York: Greenwillow Books.

In the Garden with Van Gogh by Julie Merberg and Suzanne Bober (2002). San Francisco: Chronicle Books.

Is it Red? Is It Yellow? Is It Blue? by Tana Hoban (1987). New York: Greenwillow Books.

My Crayons Talk by Patricia Hubbard (1999). New York: Henry Holt and Company.

My Many Colored Days by Dr. Seuss (1996). New York: Alfred A. Knopf.

Old Black Fly by Jim Aylesworth (1992). New York: Henry Holt and Company.

Vincent's Colors by Vincent Van Gogh (2005). San Francisco: Chronicle Books.

What is it? by Tana Hoban (1985). New York: Greenwillow Books.

What Makes a Rainbow? by Betty Ann Schwartz (2000). Los Angeles, CA.: Intervisual Books.

White Rabbit's Color Book by Alan Baker (1999). New York: Kingfisher Books.

Books About Water

Come Away From the Water, Shirley by John Burningham (1977). London: Random House Children's Books.

Jennifer's Rabbit by Tom Paxton (2001). New York: Harper Collins Publishers.

See the Ocean by Estelle Condra (1994). Nashville, TN: Ideals Children's Books.

Water Dance by Thomas Locker (1997). New York: Voyager Books Harcourt.

Books About Creativity

The Anti-Coloring Book by Susan Striker (1978). New York: Holt, Rinehart and Winston.

The Anti-Coloring Book of Masterpieces by Susan Striker (1982). New York: Holt, Rinehart and Winston.

No Good in Art by Miriam Cohen (1980). New York: Greenwillow Books.

Books About Snow

The Little Book of Snowflakes by Kenneth Libbrecht (2004). Stillwater, MN: Voyageur Press.

The Snowy Day by Ezra Jack Keats (1962). New York: Viking Press.

Alphabet Books

Alphabet Adventure by Audrey and Bruce Wood (2001) New York: The Blue Sky Press/Scholastic.

Alphabet City by Stephen T. Johnson (1995). New York: Puffin Books.

Alphabet Under Construction by Denise Fleming (2002). New York: Henry Holt and Company.

Baby Einstein: The ABC's of Art by Julie Aigner-Clark (2002). New York: Hyperion Books for Children.

Dr. Seuss's ABC by Dr. Seuss (1960). New York: Random House.

Eating the Alphabet by Lois Ehlert (1989) New York: Harcourt Children's Books.

The Graphic Alphabet by David Pelletier (1996). New York: Orchard Books.

Museum ABC by the Metropolitan Museum of Art (2002). New York: Little, Brown Young Readers.

Books About Illuminated Manuscripts

Gutenberg's Gift by Nancy Willard (1995). Baltimore, MD: Wild Honey, An Ottenheimer Publishers Company.

Marguerite Makes a Book by Bruce Robertson (1999). Los Angeles: Getty Trust Publications: The J. Paul Getty Museum.

Relevant Websites

Artsonia: http://www.artsonia.com

Association for Childhood Education International (ACEI): http://acei.org

Children's Picture Book Database at Miami University: http://www.lib.muohio.edu/pictbks

Crayola Dream Makers: http://www.crayola.com/educators/dreammakers/guide_lit.cfm

International Children Art Foundation: http://www.icaf.org

International Reading Association: http://www.reading.org

The Literacy Project: http://www.google.com/literacy

Literacy Through Art: http://www.galileo.org/projects/literacy

Literacy Today—The Art of Reading: http://www.literacytrust.org.uk/pubs/goldsmith.html

National Art Education Association: http://www.naea-reston.org

National Association for the Education of Young Children (NAEYC): http://www.naeyc.org

Reading Is Fundamental: http://www.rif.org

Reading Rockets: http://www.readingrockets.org

Swap: Art and Literacy Packet: http://sma.nebo.edu/swap/pkt/art-lit/INDEX.HTML

Tate Britain Ideas Factory: https://www.tate.org.uk/britain/ideasfactory

Teacher Art Exchange: http://www.getty.edu/education/teacherartexchange/

VSA Arts: http://www.vsarts.org

Stores and Websites to Purchase Materials

ABC Teacher's Outlet: http://www.abcteacher.com/catalog/tcr-artlit.shtml

American Science & Surplus: http://www.sciplus.com/index.cfm

Classroom Direct: http://www.classroomdirect.com

Dick Blick Art Materials: http://www.dickblick.com

Discount School Supplies: http://www.discountschoolsupply.com

Michaels: http://www.michaels.com/art/online/home

About the Authors

Kathy Danko-McGhee

Dr. Kathy Danko-McGhee is a Full Professor and the Early Childhood Art Education Coordinator at the University of Toledo. She also acts as a consultant to the Toledo Museum of Art Early Childhood Programming. Kathy was nominated as the recipient of the following awards: Art Educator of the Year in Higher Education; Outstanding Teacher of Teachers; *Who's Who of American Women*; and *Who's Who in Education.* Kathy has served as the Southeast Director of Higher Education for the National Art Education Association and currently serves on the editorial review panel for the journal, *Art Education*. She is the Arts and Young Children Editor for the *Early Childhood Education Journal*. Kathy is also on the executive board for the *International Art in Early Childhood Research Journal*. She currently serves as the president of the Toledo Association for the Education of Young Children and is a board member of the Ohio Association for the Education of the Young.

Published nationally and internationally, Dr. Danko-McGhee's main focus in research has included early childhood aesthetic preferences. Her research with young children has culminated in the book, *The Aesthetic Preferences of Young Children*, published by Mellen Press in 2000. Kathy has also presented research papers nationally and internationally, including in Australia, England, Scotland, Japan, Italy, and Greece.

Ruslan Slutsky

Dr. Ruslan Slutsky is an Associate Professor of Early Childhood Education at the University of Toledo, Judith Herb College of Education. He received his Ph.D. from the Ohio State University in 2001 in early childhood education. Dr. Slutsky is published both internationally and nationally on such topics as art and literacy, the arts and standardization, critical thinking through the arts, and preparing early childhood educators to use art in the classroom. His work has been presented internationally at conferences in England, Scotland, and most recently Australia. Dr. Slutsky's current research interests include: the Reggio Emilia approach, exploring children's art as literacy, and communities of learners.